# Find It
# Win It
# Keep It

Kate Fleming

ISBN: 978-1-5272-6323-9

First published 2020

## Contents

# About this book

Thank you for picking up a copy of my book. I've written this book for anyone who is client facing and has responsibility for winning new business from existing clients or acquiring new clients. This book will help you develop the skills and the confidence to build on the relationships you already have with your clients and prospects and to drive value from those relationships.

Before we begin, let me tell you a bit about myself and why I can help you achieve your sales and client management goals. I've worked in the professional services sector for 20 years. During that time I've sold professional services to senior buyers, helped others to sell professional services and undertaken a number of research studies to understand better how clients buy professional services. This book is a practical guide to the skills you need to successfully navigate your journey through an increasingly complex sales process from contact to contract.

I started in the professional services sector as a marketing director for one of the leading commercial law firms in Manchester. While in this role it became increasingly obvious that the market for legal services was getting tougher – simply building relationships and waiting for enough of the right work to come through the door would not be a sustainable model in the future. So, I set up my own business, working with lawyers, surveyors, accountants and others in the professional service firms to help them to develop their sales and client management capability. Of course in those days "sales" was a dirty word and we had to use terms such as "business development" or "practice development". Today, the willingness to embrace sales, recognise good practice and learn the skills required is recognised as a key differentiator in a highly competitive and mature market for professional services.

This book is a truly practical guide, based on tried and tested techniques, to help you win more business. There are three principle stages in the pursuit of new business – finding new business opportunities, winning new business opportunities and keeping the business; developing and growing it. At each of these stages there are tools and techniques that will enable you to manage your sales opportunities more effectively.

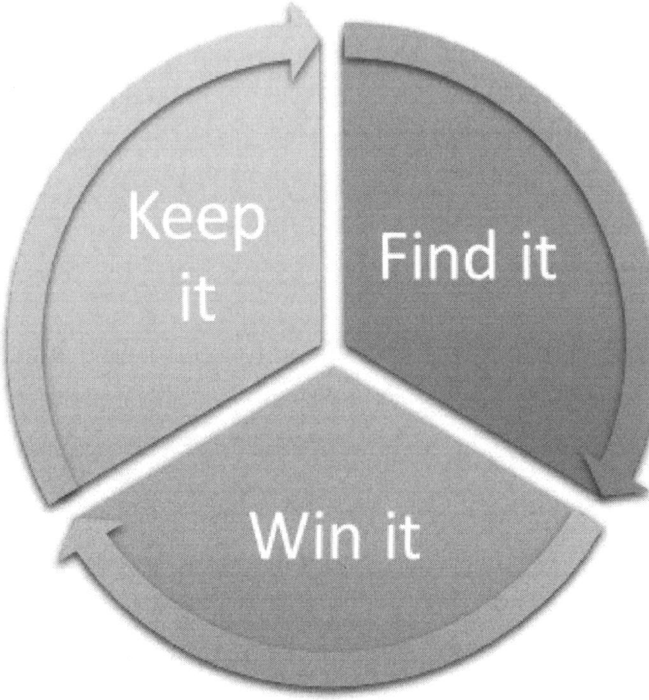


As I take you through your sales journey, I'll introduce you to tools and techniques that will help you to make decisions and then plan and implement your sales strategy.

# Introduction – leveraging value from relationships

Business development in the professional services sector comes with its own challenges. In this sector, the model for sales and client management is unique, in that fee earners who do the work, also need to win the business. The individuals who deliver services to clients – legal, financial, consultancy services – are also responsible for acquiring new clients, and for looking after and nurturing client relationships. Selling business and professional services is different from selling any kind of product. Buyers cannot see, touch, or feel what you are selling, and often professionals that should sell (or must sell) have difficulty coming to grips with being "in sales" when they never thought they would be. It is not what they signed up for.

Another complication is that the market for professional services is oversupplied and under differentiated in the eyes of buyers, which means establishing and sustaining a competitive advantage is tough. Without a doubt, selling skills – the ability to build relationships and turn those relationships into profitable work, is now the longest lasting and most sustainable source of competitive advantage for professional service firms.

**Overcoming the roadblocks**

In my work with professional firms, I spend time with individual fee earners and groups of people, and I believe there are seven principle roadblocks that you need to overcome to improve your sales effectiveness.

1. **Resistance to the idea of selling**

*"No one told me I had to sell!"*

The first difficulty is with the model for sales and client management that we see in most professional firms. The majority of individuals don't see themselves as salespeople. Many professional advisers feel uncomfortable and regard sales as a necessary evil, preferring to concentrate on using their expertise and technical knowledge. Understandably they would argue that they trained as a lawyer, an accountant, a surveyor or management consultant, not a salesperson.

In my experience, fee earners often perceive sales people as pushy and just trying to sell their services, whether or not these services are relevant or of value to the client – in other words *"I have something I want you to buy and I'll attempt to persuade you to do that"*, which is seen as the individual driving their own agenda and not always in the best interest of the client.

Most professional advisers, however, are keen to become their clients' "Trusted Advisers" and valued business partners, which requires a high degree of client centricity and this is in fact the basis of sales effectiveness. In reality, the act of selling, when done well, adds significant value to clients. A well-planned sales conversation can help even sophisticated buyers make smarter decisions.

In this book I want to show you that the most effective approach to sales is, in fact, another form of advice. Effective sellers focus on their client's business, they help their clients to understand their current and future challenges, quantify and prioritise their needs, explore alternative options and manage risk. Clients need to achieve consensus and agreement with internal colleagues, and effective sellers help them to do this. Clients tell us that what they value most is when their advisers teach them things they didn't know (maybe about what is happening in their sector or what they have learnt from what competitors do) or provide an alternative perspective for a client. This level of client centricity and ability to guide clients' thinking is, in fact, the basis of effective selling.

2. **Meetings concentrate on technical knowledge and expertise**

A significant majority of professional advisers believe their principle value to their clients is their technical knowledge and expertise – their self-esteem and confidence is built around this. So, when preparing for meetings and indeed during meetings, they tend to focus on *"telling the client what they can do"* and not *"exploring with the client what is going on in their business and how they can help".* Although individuals are quite capable of asking questions and showing interest in their client's business, in a sales situation, which for some people is quite stressful, I see many fee earners default to talking about their services and what they do. This is what they feel comfortable talking about, rather than engaging the client in a true dialogue about their business.

The other behaviour I see in client meetings is the client taking control and asking questions. Most professional advisers feel quite comfortable with this, as it feels more like the advisory conversation they are used to i.e. they are providing the client with the information they ask for and this conversation, led by the client, is usually focused on exploring their expertise and technical knowledge. This client-led, technically focused conversation should not be confused with an effective sales conversation – more on this in chapters 6 & 7.

**Professional advisers concentrate on service delivery and miss important business development opportunities**

Day-to-day service delivery meetings are an ideal time to identify other opportunities. I call this "sales through service" and it is a particularly valuable sales opportunity, especially in the current environment when getting access to decision-makers is so difficult. Furthermore, it is a smart use of time, when so many fee earners struggle to find time to both do the work and win the work.

However, routine client meetings are rarely used in this way. Implementation, whether it is a specific transaction, a project or a piece of advisory work, means that individuals are spending significant amounts of time with clients. I always encourage fee earners to use this time to move beyond just the matter in hand and explore other opportunities. There is a health warning here though!

1. You need to get agreement from the client that you'd like some time to talk about other things and you might let them know what you want to talk about.
2. Focus the conversation on how you can help, not what you do.

Implementation is also a time where individuals may well have access to, or be able to find out about other stakeholders elsewhere in the business, who they and their colleagues may need to reach out to, in order to develop other new business opportunities. Implementation and involvement in one part of the business may well highlight problems and needs elsewhere, so staying alert to these other opportunities is important. Fee earners may well become aware of changes, such as change of personnel, new strategic goals, changes in business structure, problems with other advisers, however, these golden opportunities to identify the next piece of work are often missed because individuals are focused on delivery.

### 3. Reward and recognition frequently not aligned to sales

I frequently have conversations with fee earners to explore how they can use routine meetings more effectively and not miss opportunities for further work. The common reason I'm given for not spending time exploiting the business development value from routine client meetings is that in most professional firms, individuals are generally rewarded and recognised for achieving their own fee earning and billing targets. This is a classic case of what gets measured gets done. Where individuals are rewarded and recognised for cross selling and developing new opportunities then we see a different pattern of behaviour.

4. **Fee earners in professional firms think they know more about their clients' businesses than they actually do**

Most professional firms are structured around practice areas as opposed to sectors or industry groups. Having said that there are some firms who have evolved their route to market via sectors very effectively, i.e. there are resources aligned to the sector, individuals are aligned to a sector, KPIs are applied to the sector and people will describe their sector role rather than their area of technical expertise.

Where the firm is organised around practice groups, however, individuals tend to focus on developing their technical expertise and this can lead to a blind spot in their understanding of the client's world. This results in fee earners making assumptions about their clients' needs and priorities and they end up telling clients what they need rather than sharing insights, exploring and listening to the client.

When asked what buyers of professional services value most, sector knowledge is always high on their list. The problem is that a lot of professional advisers don't have as much knowledge as clients would like or they don't use the knowledge they have sufficiently well enough for the benefit of their clients.

5. **Fee earners in professional firms lack the experience to engage effectively with senior stakeholders in client organisations**

The sales landscape for professional services has changed dramatically in recent years. One of the most significant changes is the number of stakeholders influencing and making decisions. Today's business to business (B2B) purchases (and that includes professional services) are made by large and diverse groups of stakeholders. Decisions are no longer made by one or two people, fee earners are now dealing with "buying groups" and many of these buying groups include board level executives. The role of board level executives is generally to scrutinise decisions, to evaluate and on occasions authorise the choices of others. So, while it is unlikely they will make decisions, they can say "NO". Furthermore, individuals who are well connected to board level executives often have more influence with the buying group.

Many senior advisers in professional firms have the necessary seniority and positional authority to engage with board level executives. However, many individuals will not have gained the skills required to engage with senior stakeholders because most of their time will have been spent in service delivery and implementation. Being able to engage on the broader business issues and think like a board level executive is key to successful engagement at this level. More to come in chapter 9.

### 6. Too focused on the relationship and too reactive

Any successful sales strategy is built on a bedrock of really strong client relationships. Clients do business with people they like and trust, clients will not want to work with individuals without that trust and comfort. In my experience, in many professional firms there is still a belief that having a good relationship will result in enough work – be that new clients, repeat business or referrals. However, while a good relationship is critical, it is not enough, and other skills are needed to leverage the full value from a relationship.

I make a distinction between relationship skills and selling skills. Relationship skills focus on building rapport, credibility and integrity, which are the key ingredients of trust. Building relationships requires an investment in time and must not just be about business. Selling skills are more focused on results and should concentrate on driving value from relationships. It's important not to focus only on defending the relationship, but promoting growth as well.

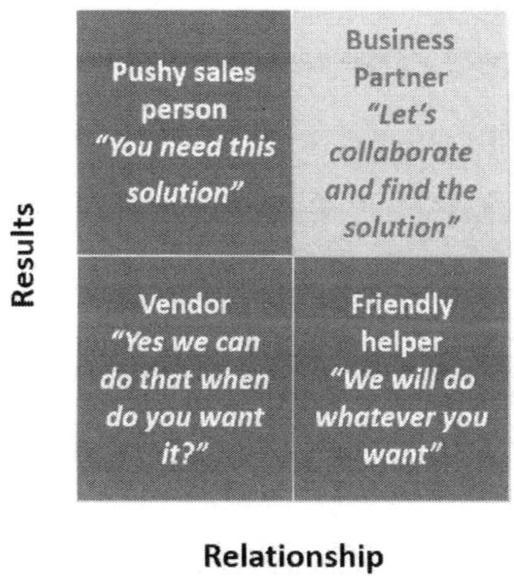


fig 1. Relationship v Results

# FIND IT

# Chapter 1

## The seller's landscape – what high performing sellers do differently

This book is about how professional advisers can be successful at winning business. So, it's important that I put some context around it, look at how the market for professional services has changed in recent years and understand what this means for professional advisers who are out there trying to attract new clients and win new business.

There was a time when professional advisers could be pretty confident that if they did a good job and looked after their clients, they would get a steady flow of work and a clutch of referrals which would provide enough work for them and a few people in their team. But the world has moved on. The landscape is a lot more complex and challenging, and buyers are considerably more sophisticated and demanding.

In this chapter I want to look at how Business to Business (B2B) buyer behaviour and preferences have changed in how they want suppliers to engage with them and how they make decisions. We call this "The Buyer's Journey". What sets high performing sellers apart is that they understand and know how to work with clients through their journey.

**Buyers are less accessible**

To start with, buyers rely more on technology for their information than human interaction, as was the case in the past. Getting access to buyers presents a real challenge for professional advisers, yet without access it's very difficult to influence clients' buying decisions. Today's professional advisers need to provide clients with a great buying experience throughout their buying journey – one which is personalised, insightful and offers something they can't get from their other sources of information. High performing sellers offer relevant thought leadership, insight and relevant expertise at every stage of the buyer's journey to the point at which a decision is made. In short, while they are not the main source of information, they need to be the source of the **most valuable** information.

Two years ago, I ran a focus group with 30 buyers of professional services. I asked the question "What is it that your advisers do that you really value and that you'd like them to do more of?" Without exception they said, *"Tell us about the things we should be thinking about that we're not", "Tell us what's coming over the horizon that we need to be aware of", "Help us interpret the wealth of information we have and tell us what's important"*. They also said professional advisers that offered them a different perspective or disrupted their current viewpoint really delivered value.

The Corporate Executive Board, formerly part of Harvard Business School, ran a study and identified that one of the factors which distinguished high performing B2B sellers was that they "educated" clients, which is consistent with the findings from my focus group.

Put simply, professional advisers who engage with their clients and prospects and provide a great buying experience throughout their buying journey, will attract more clients and win more business. Individuals who only engage at the end of their buying journey, when the opportunity to pitch arises, may well be at a disadvantage.

### More internal people added to the decision-making process

One of the most significant changes in the last few years is the number of people who are involved in making purchasing decisions. Decisions made at middle management level, that may have involved two or three people a few years ago, now involve up to six people and that may include scrutiny from the C-suite. This is because there is generally less appetite for risk and a more consensual and collaborative business culture. So, high performing sellers devote time to developing the right relationships and engaging with the right people throughout the buyer's journey, to ensure they have maximum influence and opportunity to win the business. The reality is that you are now dealing with buying groups who make, influence and scrutinise decisions, and whose members have different preferences and priorities, thus making decision-making increasingly complex and difficult to influence.

### More time spent researching before purchasing

Buyers' purchasing processes have changed in recent years. In addition to the larger and more formal buying groups I described above, far more time is being spent researching and evaluating potential purchases. People no longer say, "Hey, this is a great solution, it's in my budget, let's do it!" They need to look at the potential return they are going to get and the impact any decision may have elsewhere, and what they need to do to successfully implement solutions. All of this slows decision-making down, increases the risk of "no decision" and generally creates more hoops for buyers to jump through to reach the point of making a decision. There is no doubt about it, decision-making is materially slower than it was just a few years back.

**They want to engage with suppliers who understand their business and know the sector**

*"It's not what you sell, it's how you sell" – VP, Gartner research*

Increasingly the factor which differentiates high performing sellers is the research they do and their knowledge and understanding of the client's business. Furthermore, experience, understanding and track record working in the client's market sector will definitely give individuals a head start with clients as this is now really important to buyers making complex B2B purchasing decisions.

The experience clients have with suppliers through their buying journey is increasingly the driver of client loyalty and key decision criteria.

In the focus group I ran two years ago, I also asked buyers why they chose the supplier they chose in the recent purchasing decisions they had made. Here are some of the responses.

**The mindset of high performing sellers**

As well as understanding the seller's landscape and how buyer behaviour has evolved, it is important to understand the mindset with which you need to approach sales. I've distilled this information into an easy to understand framework to act as a guide to help individuals develop the mindset needed to become high performing sellers.

I've spent many years selling high value professional services to senior buyers and working with individuals in professional firms helping them to win business. The mindset of winners is very different from those who are average performers. Over the years I've captured the data from my own experience and from the experience of helping others and identified that there are 6 distinguishing characteristics or mindset which set high performing sellers apart from core or average performers.

| Curious | Control | Conscientious | Clarity | Courageous | Critical |
|---|---|---|---|---|---|
| interested in what is going on in the client's world | proactively engages with clients and doesn't just wait for inbound enquiries | takes responsibility for attracting clients and new business | written communication is clear and focused on the client | willing to disrupt the client's status quo to explore business improvement | critical of own performance and constantly seeking improvements |
| uses a strong questioning style to uncover key information and influence client's needs | prepares and plans for each meeting and sets realistic objectives | see themselves as accountable both to the firm and the client for the required results | presentations are well prepared and well planned to achieve objectives | asks the difficult questions and is happy to take calculated take risks | does not accept information at face value without exploring further |
| doesn't make assumptions without testing them first | guides the sales conversation and structures the meeting to focus on the right things | totally reliable and consistent and works collaboratively with others for the good of the client | has a clear vision of what can be achieved in developing individual clients and for client acquisition | engages with the client on their agenda and creates client value not just communicates value | actively seeks feedback from others in order to improve performance |
| focused on how they can help the client not what they do | maintains the momentum to keep the opportunity alive | engages effectively with internal teams to deliver results | persuasively articulates goals and strategies to others and builds commitment | consistently focused on business improvement for the client | applies high level of critical thinking to understand their clients' world and help others to understand it |

fig 2. Mindset of high performing sellers

**Summary of what you have learnt in this chapter**

B2B buyer behaviour has evolved and it is critical for firms to keep up with these changes and stay close to the decision-makers throughout the buying journey. The importance of knowing your buyers, tailoring experiences and customising content and staying engaged in a way that is relevant throughout the buying journey is critical to your success.

# Chapter 2

## Targeting new clients

As I have highlighted a number of times, the model for sales and client management in the professional services sector is unique, in that those who win the work also have to do the work. Building and managing a pipeline of opportunities, while managing a practice of active and demanding clients, often creates conflicting priorities and is a challenge to manage. Individuals who have responsibility for winning work, need to work smart if they are going to balance these differing priorities.

Success at winning business means you need to invest your time and effort in organisations which, in the short/medium and long term, will be profitable clients for you. In this chapter I will explore how to make objective and accurate decisions about which clients and prospects to target, to enable you to invest your time and effort in the right opportunities.

Existing clients, lapsed clients and new prospects are all sources of new business and it will not surprise anyone to hear that existing clients are the most profitable source of new business; however, that value is rarely leveraged as effectively as it could be. Not all the clients and prospects on your list are equally valuable. You should take on and invest time and effort in those targets for which your talents and efforts will be appreciated and rewarded. Furthermore, if you spend time on poor and unprofitable opportunities, there is every chance you will lose out on other more profitable opportunities.

Most firms carry out broad brush marketing in the hope that the clients they want to work for will reveal themselves. An effective marketing campaign is critical to raise awareness and strengthen a firm's sales environment. However, alongside this activity, it is also important that you have a plan of exactly which organisations you would like to work for and who in those organisations you need to get to know.

If you simply rely on inbound enquiries and wait for opportunities to come to you, at worst you won't have enough work, and at best, you'll have no control over the work that comes in – and the work that comes in may not be the work you want.

There are three questions you need to answer to help you plan your targeting strategy.

- Which organisations are attractive to us?
- In which organisations could we establish a competitive advantage?
- Are there any organisations that we are currently investing time in that will not bring us a good return on investment (ROI)?

This is called **"qualification"** and a rigorous approach to qualification will ensure you get the best ROI on your sales effort. You need to qualify the clients and prospects you want to target as well as the opportunities that come to you. Just because a client presents you with an opportunity or invites you to pitch, does not mean it is a good opportunity for you. It is important to qualify-out as well as qualify-in.

So how do you pick the clients where you are likely to get the greatest ROI for effort and time?

There are two measures that will help you to pick your target clients and which you should invest your resources in.

- **Accessibility criteria** – Those criteria that help you to assess if you are well placed to win business and win it over your competitors;
- **Attractiveness criteria** – Those criteria that make a client attractive to you.

When assessing whether they should target a client, many people focus only on the **ATTRACTIVENESS** criteria and so the best opportunities may be missed.

**Typical factors for assessing ACCESSIBILITY**

- You know their company & have experience of their sector.
- You can gain access to and influence key stakeholders.
- They have a track record of using similar firms.
- You have a good reputation e.g. positive client feedback reports.
- The client's requirements match your firm's strengths.
- There is a lack of competition.

**Typical factors for assessing ATTRACTIVENESS**

- The potential revenues are good, now and in the future.
- They outsource the services we can provide.
- It's a good client, which might open doors to others.
- It's a growing company and/or regulatory or legislative change.
- There is an opportunity to cross sell other services.
- They are a client in our target sectors/geography.

You then need to create a Targeting Scorecard to help you make decisions about which clients to target. There are two tables below, which you can use to plan which clients or prospects you want to target.

- Scoring guidelines
- Targeting scorecard

**Scoring guidelines** (this table illustrates a set of factors which may be used to assess attractiveness and a series of measures that could be used to score each one).

**Attractiveness –** Criteria which makes the client attractive to us:

| Criteria | 10 | 5 | 0 |
|---|---|---|---|
| **Potential revenue** | *Revenue levels will vary* | *Firm to firm so you need* | *decide what is right for you* |
| **Is there an opportunity to cross sell a range of services?** | 1-2 practice groups work for the client and we expect to be able to sell in a number of our other practice groups | 3 or more practice groups work for the client. Some opportunity to sell in other practice groups | The firm provides a full range of services or we know they like to use different lawyers to provide different services |
| **Are they a client in our target sector/ geography** | They are in both target sector and geography | Sector/or geography | Neither sector nor geography |
| **Are they a client in our target sector/ geography** | Sector and geography | Sector/or geography | Neither sector nor geography |
| **Good client that will open other opportunities?** | Client is a strategically important client with a good reputation | Client is a strong regional client with a good reputation | Client is national but not well known |
| **Growth and/or regulatory or legislative change?** | Highly acquisitive and/ or in an environment of change | Some acquisitions & regulatory and/or legislative change | Static growth – no acquisitions planned & little change |
| **Do they outsource the services we provide?** | No legal team and all legal requirements are outsourced. No established panel | Legal team but client also uses a preferred list of external lawyers when outsourcing work | Well-established legal team and the use of external legal providers is by exception |

**Accessibility –** Criteria which mean we are well placed to win business and win it over competitors:

| Criteria | 10 | 5 | 0 |
|---|---|---|---|
| Do we have strong sector expertise and knowledge of their company | We are recognised by them as experts in their sector and have established a high level of knowledge about the company | We know their sector but we are not recognised as sector experts. We have limited knowledge of the company | We don't know the sector well and we have very limited knowledge of the company |
| Do we know key stakeholders and can access them easily? | We have multiple relationships with key stakeholders in different parts of the organisation and can gain access | A number of relationships but no senior stakeholders | Just one or more relationships, mostly at a junior level |
| Do they have a track record of using similar firms? | Uses similar firms for a wide range of services | Occasionally use firms similar to us | Don't use firms that match our profile |
| Do we have a good reputation, good feedback/NPS score from client listening? | We are the "go-to" firm for a number of their stakeholders. Client feedback is excellent, and we have an NPS of 9 or 10 | On some occasions we may be the firm of choice. Client feedback generally good though some areas for improvement have been identified | Use us on an ad hoc basis with similar or little differentiation from competing firms. Some improvements identified in client feedback |
| Do their requirements match our strengths? | Their current and future requirements match the areas where they see us as strong | Some of their requirements match areas where we are strong but there are gaps | One or more competitor's strengths match their requirements |
| How strong is the competition? | They use other firms, but we are the preferred supplier. No in-house team | We are one of a number of firms they use. Small in-house team | A number of in-house lawyers and they use a number of law firms but we are not the preferred supplier |

## Targeting scorecard

| Client: ____________________ | Weighting (scores should add up to 10) | Score (1=low, 10=high) | |
|---|---|---|---|
| **Accessibility Criteria** | | | **Additional comments** |
| • How well do we know this company? | 4 | 5 | We've worked for one division of this company and know their business quite well, but we don't know the other business divisions so well |
| • How strong is our knowledge and experience of their sector? | 3 | 9 | They recognise us as experts and often seek our advice on sector matters |
| • Do we have strong relationships with, and can we gain access to key stakeholders? | 1 | 6 | We have strong relationships at middle management level but not in the C-suite and we know they are involved in decisions |
| • Have we received positive client feedback (our reputation)? | 0.5 | 8 | Good client feedback, a few minor improvements required and an NPS of 9 |
| • Have we got a track record of success with them? | 0.5 | 9 | We have been able to demonstrate improved efficiencies and reduced risk through our work with them |
| • How strong is the competition? | 1 | 10 | We are their preferred supplier and they use a number of other external law firms |
| **Total score divided by 6** | **10** | **7.8** | |

### Mapping your scores

Below is a **Client Development Matrix**. Map each of your target clients, based on the targeting scorecard and then you can plan the most appropriate and effective sales and client development strategy for your portfolio of clients and prospects.

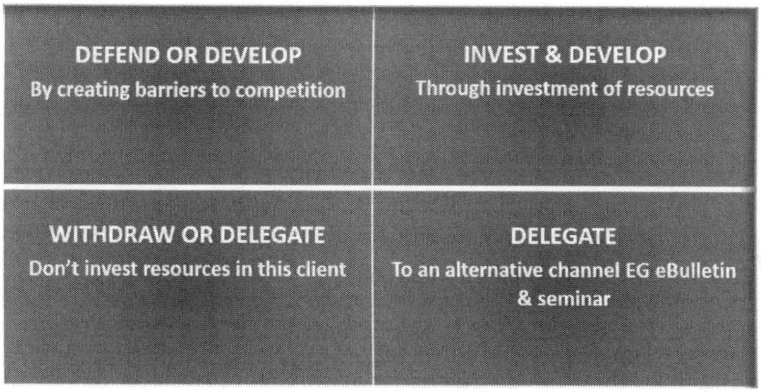


fig 3. Client Development Matrix

### Strategies for developing clients and winning new business

**Invest and develop** – Clients and prospects that you map into this part of the client development matrix are those clients where you should be investing your sales and client development resources. It is also the group of clients where you need to have plans which are closely managed and measured, to ensure you achieve the best return on the investment of your resources. These are the clients and prospects where you should spend more time in one-to-one, face-to-face activities. These are the clients and prospects where you should invest in more personalised campaigns in order to win their business.

**Delegate** – The clients and prospects that you map onto this part of your sales and client development matrix are those which are attractive to you. However, your ability to establish competitive advantage or win business ahead of competitors will be difficult. Nevertheless, you do not want to cast them adrift and lose touch altogether. Businesses change all the time and it may be that the clients and prospects in this part of the matrix become more accessible to you in time. It is therefore important to maintain contact and continue to build and develop relationships. A programme of networking events will enable you to do this cost effectively and can contribute enormous value to your sales and client development programme.

**Defend or develop** – Clients and prospects that you map onto this part of your sales and client development matrix are those that may already be long-standing clients, and important clients. You will probably have a strong track record and well-established relationships with key stakeholders. The chances are that you are providing a range of services and may well be the only firm of professional advisers they use for your type of services. It is highly likely that you and indeed a number of colleagues may be their "Go-To" advisers. If there is no opportunity to develop this client further, your best strategy is to defend the business you have. This means staying close, being proactive and continually looking for ways to help your client do business better. The biggest risk in managing these long-established relationships is complacency, which allows competitors in by the back door.

**Withdraw or delegate** – If you are absolutely certain that the score for both attractiveness and accessibility is low, then there is no justifiable business case for investing any resource or effort in these clients and they should either be removed from your target list, or at very least remain on the list of invitees for your programme of networking events.

### Qualifying inbound enquiries

So far, in this chapter, I have explained how to establish a rigorous methodology for selecting the clients where you are most likely to get a return on the investment of your sales activity and resources. However, you also need to apply the same rigour to inbound enquiries and opportunities. The sales model in professional firms means that a large proportion of the sales opportunities that individuals and teams pursue are inbound enquiries.

Inbound enquiries and opportunities come in many forms. Enquiries may come in as a formal request for proposal (RFP) or as less-formal expressions of interest in your services.

There are two common traps which I have seen many individuals, or indeed teams, falling into:

1. Because an individual has been approached, they may be overly optimistic about the likelihood of success.
2. A reluctance to say "no" to opportunities for fear of offending the person or people who have requested their participation in a tender. *"We can't really say no as they have invited us, and it wouldn't look very good if we didn't take part".*

Responding to inbound enquiries in either of these ways results in the potential waste of significant resource and potentially missing out on other more profitable opportunities. It is equally important to apply rigour to your qualification of inbound enquiries as it is to the list of clients and prospects you plan to target. The methodology set out in this chapter is also highly effective in helping you with your "Go-No-Go" decisions.

**Summary of what you have learnt in this chapter**

- **Don't rely on inbound enquiries –** you may be very clear on the sort of clients you want to work for but relying on inbound enquiries and opportunities may not produce enough of the clients you want.
- **Be rigorous** in how you make decisions on which clients and prospects to target.
- Target clients on **ATTRACTIVENESS and ACCESSIBILITY**
- Create a **targeting scorecard** and use the **client development matrix** to help you plan your strategy.
- **You can use the same methodology to qualify inbound enquiries.** This will help you apply rigour to your Go-No-Go decisions.

# Chapter 3

## The power of word of mouth – how to avoid the cold call

If you are reading this book, I imagine it's because you are actively involved, or planning to be involved, in winning new business for your firm. In this chapter you will learn how you can develop an effective referral system for generating new opportunities from your network and avoid having to cold call.

Whatever your practice area or the nature of your work, it is highly likely that an important part of your role is to develop new business opportunities. Whether the focus of your activity is on winning more business from existing clients or acquiring new clients, getting in front of the right decision-makers is always a challenge. This is particularly true in today's business environment when stakeholders are less and less accessible and less inclined to see you. It may be that you have had some success with cold calling – and well done if you have – but the chances are, that more often than not, attempts to cold call lead to "no reply" to emails you send and the dreaded voicemail when you try to call. This leaves you feeling frustrated and discouraged. So, what's the answer?

There are many sales strategies that you can adopt, but I would say that for getting to meet new prospects and client contacts, the most effective is referral selling. If you can develop an effective system for building a pipeline of new prospects and new business opportunities, from referrals, it means you won't have to cold call.

At this point, I'd like to clarify the meaning of referral selling in this context. There are many official sources of referral that professional firms use to generate business, e.g. The National Accident Helpline is a source of referral used by a number of personal injury law firms. Equally in business to consumer (B2C) sales and marketing, a number of businesses establish systems whereby they incentivise customers to make referrals. These are valuable sources of new business for the organisations that use them, however these activities are not what I am focusing on in this chapter. The referral system I am talking about is based on leveraging the good will of the people in your network you know and with whom you have good relationships and who respect what you do.

Most people involved in sales recognise the value of referrals. Referrals are a significantly more cost-effective way to develop business than cold calling, and of course the comfort factor is much higher too.

Apart from the hardened sales professionals and serious rainmakers, most people have a passive approach to referrals. If someone offers to refer us, we are likely to grab the opportunity and be very grateful, but somehow our natural reserve prevents us from being any more proactive than this.

Yet having a good referral system is a great way to get to know new people and build a pipeline of prospects. So put your reserve aside and remember the people that you have good relationships with are only too happy to introduce and recommend you to others; you just need the courage and confidence to ask others to help you build your business.

If you need more convincing of the power of word of mouth, look at the findings below which come from a number of articles which report on the value of referral business.

- 65% of new business comes from referrals – *The New York Times*
- 92% of respondents trust referrals from people they know – *Nielson*
- The lifetime value of a new referral customer is 16% higher – *Wharton School of Business*
- 83% of consumers are willing to refer after a positive experience – yet only 29% actually do – *Texas Tech University*

These stats don't tell you how to build a referral programme, but they do show the value, if done right.

When speaking to people involved in sales, they will always acknowledge the importance of referrals, saying that opportunities introduced this way have a higher rate of conversion and will often convert faster.

If you are looking to build a practice or simply contribute more effectively to your firm's sales effort, there are a few simple things you can do to build your own referral system. Here are some simple tips and techniques to help you build a successful referral system.

**A case in point...**

When I was running my business and responsible for building our client base and selling training and consultancy services to senior buyers, I decided to target the Republic of Ireland. The professional services market was significant, and at the time there were no companies specialising in the sector and providing the services that I did. I got a lucky break and began working with The Law Society of Ireland. My contact there was very well connected and influential in the legal market, and so after I had run a number of projects and I had built my credibility with her, I sat down with her and explained that I wanted to build my practice in the Republic of Ireland and asked her if she

> could help me. She proved to be a very helpful referee. Initially, she introduced me to a couple of the big law firms in Dublin and I went on to do work for them and this became my platform for building my pipeline of work as they too were willing to make introductions and referrals.
>
> Within 2 years I was working for seven professional firms in Ireland. Initially, I worked with law firms but then moved into property and accountancy. At one point, Ireland represented 20% of our revenue for a period of about three years.

**Developing your referral system**

*"If you want to go fast, go alone. If you want to go far, go with others"*
*- African proverb*

If you want to start being more proactive and effective at winning business via your network of referrers, you need to develop an organised and systematic approach to generating opportunities this way. When I talk about generating business through referral, as I said in a previous paragraph, I am not talking about the relationships some firms establish with official sources of referral such as the National Accident Helpline that some personal injury law firms use. I am talking about a more informal, though highly effective, source of introduction based on the relationships you have with people in your network.

The first thing you need to establish is a clear picture of who is in your network. Most of us have a network of people we know that is far larger than we think, so a good place to start is to make a list of all your "Network Sources". A point of clarification, when we talk about your network in this context, it is people you KNOW and who KNOW YOU.

Look at the following groups of people to get an idea of the size of your network and your potential sources of referral.

- Clients
- Colleagues
- Alumni (people you may have previously worked with )
- University and school friends and contacts
- Intermediaries and other advisers
- Sports clubs and groups

You may have an extensive number of contacts on LinkedIn, and this is important but many of the people you are connected to on LinkedIn and other social media channels, you may not know at all and therefore it would not be appropriate to ask for referrals or introductions. A final thought on your LinkedIn contacts. What you may find, as you go through this exercise, are people with whom you are connected but who you don't know and who you may want to ask others in your network to introduce you to, so add these people to your target list.

Most people have a large network of business and social contacts. The key question is are you spending time with those people in your network that can deliver greatest value and can give you help in your business?

To start with you need to understand the **CURRENT REFERRAL VALUE** of your network and then identify how you can **ENHANCE THE VALUE**. To assess the value of your network, you can use two criteria:

**Capability** – The ability of your network contacts to introduce you to others or refer work to you. To assess capability, you need to ask 3 questions:

- How large is THEIR network?
- How influential are they in their network?
- Do they know people that you want to know?

**Willingness** – The willingness of your network contacts to introduce you to others or refer work to you.

- Are they willing to introduce you and/refer you to business opportunities?
- Do they have a sense of obligation – have you helped them or introduced them to opportunities?
- Are they happy to share information and spend time with you?

Then on a scale of 1–10 you need to score the people in your network to help you identify where the value of your network currently lies. This will also give you a clearer picture of where you need to focus to enhance the value of your network.

| | Contact 1<br>1=low<br>10=high | Contact 2<br>1=low<br>10=high | Contact 3<br>1=low<br>10=high | Contact 3<br>1=low<br>10=high |
|---|---|---|---|---|
| **Capability**<br>They have a large network of people.<br>They have a network of people I want to meet<br>They are influential in their network | 10 | 7 | 9 | 4 |
| **Willingness**<br>They are willing to share information<br>They are willing to make introductions<br>There is an obligation (e.g. I have made introductions or helped in some way) | 8 | 4 | 4 | 3 |

fig 4. Networking Scoring Matrix

Once you have completed this scoring exercise, you can map each contact on to **The Network Value Matrix** and start making your plans.

This can be a useful exercise to help you benchmark what you anecdotally know about the value of your network.

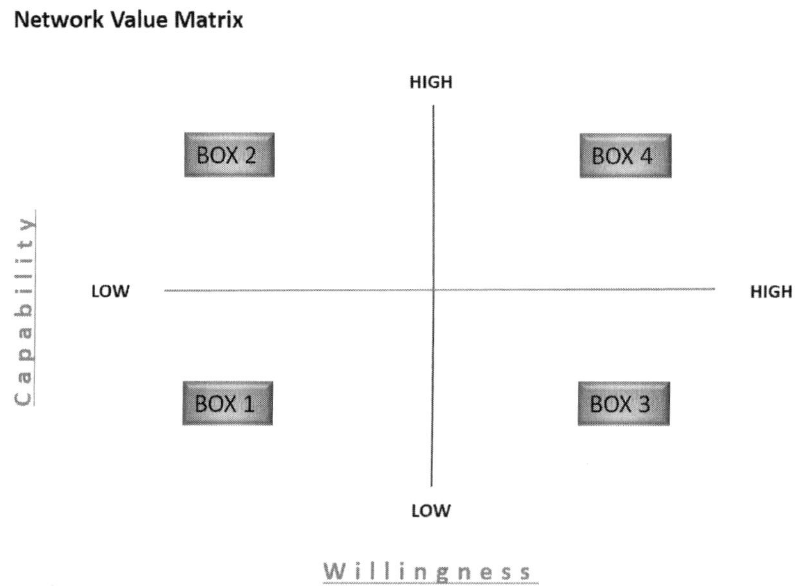


fig 5. Networking Value Matrix

**Enhancing the value of your network**

Once you have a better understanding of your network and where the value lies, you can start to plan strategies to help you enhance the value of your network.

**Contacts who are high on willingness and high on capability –** These are your key contacts and probably the people you are closest to. You may already be getting referrals and introductions, but you may still be relying on them to think of you and remembering to make a referral? These are the people who should be in the forefront of your mind to ask for help, when you are attempting to meet new people. However, it is important that you find ways to reciprocate. There is a limit to how many times you can ask your key contacts for introductions, if you don't find a way that you can help them in return. Returning their help may come in a number of formats e.g. one of my clients with whom I regularly work has always been extremely supportive and willing to make introductions – in fact the CRV (client referral value) was higher than the fees. However, I started to feel awkward asking, as I had not been able to reciprocate. Then I learnt of a job which would be a great move for him. I introduced my client to the recruiter and hey presto – he got the job!

Your current and former clients are your best source of referrals because they know you and have first-hand experience of the value you deliver. They choose to do business with you, so why wouldn't they introduce you and recommend you to others?

**Contacts who are high on capability but low on willingness –** These are an important group of people in your network as they can potentially introduce you and plug you in to some really useful opportunities. In professional firms, it is often your colleagues that fall into this box. Lack of willingness often arises as a result of "lack of trust" or lack of understanding and knowledge about what you do and how you can help their clients. It is easy to assume that colleagues will automatically be happy to make introductions to the firm's clients they look after. Sadly, this is a flawed assumption. As you will have no doubt discovered, colleagues can be very reluctant to help and this is because they often feel a huge sense of ownership of the client relationships they look after and won't put themselves or the relationship at risk. To build the value of your network with contacts in this part of the matrix you need to build relationships with them, so that they trust you and know that you won't damage the relationship they have with the people you want introductions to. You also need to educate them about how you can help – telling them about what you do, providing evidence of how you have helped clients, which we call "social proof".

### Contacts who are low on capability and low on willingness

There may well be people in your network that you know and with whom you have a good relationship, but you don't know their network value. These are the people you may want to find out more about in terms of their network value.

### Asking for referrals

Once you have a sense of who is who in your network and who knows people you want to know and would be willing to introduce you to their contacts, it is time to start asking for introductions. There is a way to do this and a way not to do this.

Most people feel uncomfortable about asking for referrals and are often vague in the way they ask.

*"Hey, if you hear of anyone looking for what I do, will you introduce me?"*

Your clients, colleagues and others in your network, even the most well-intentioned are busy and are unlikely to remember once the conversation is over. In my experience there are two factors that are critical to establishing your referral system as a way to build your sales pipeline.

1. Be very clear on who you want to meet and why – how you can help not what you want to sell.
2. Make it easy for your referee. If someone is putting themselves out to introduce you, you cannot expect them to do the thinking. Be prepared to draft an introductory email for your referee. Of course, if you do this it's important that your referee can make any amendments to make it their own. If you've done the heavy lifting around the thinking of why your referee's contact should meet you, that won't be too onerous.

Another approach to asking for referrals is less specific. It may be that you want to reach out to a specific company or meet people in a specific geographical region or market sector. The referral request is then less specific.

*"Venture is a large developer and I would be keen to get to know the company – do you know people there? Who should I be speaking to?"*

Finally, generating referrals is a highly effective way to support your cross selling and client development activity. If there are other parts of a client organisation you want to get to know, your existing contacts may well be able to make introductions to their colleagues in other parts of the business. The same principle applies – make it easy and be clear on how you can help that part of the organisation you want to get access to.

**Making referral requests**

*"I was wondering if you could help me please."*

*"Perhaps you could give me some advice on how I might reach out to...."*

*"I am keen to meet people at xyz PLC and I know that you know people there – would you be able to help set up some meetings, please. Let me tell you how I can help?"*

*"I am keen to increase my portfolio of consultancy work – would you be able to introduce me to some of the directors you know, please. I think I have some interesting ideas about how I can help them identify new acquisitions, which I know is important?"*

*"I know you know Alain Honour. I am keen to meet him as I think I can help him with some ideas to help his customers. Would you be willing to introduce me?"*

*"You have a colleague in the corporate department, would you be happy to introduce me?"*

*"Can I say you suggested I should call?" "Can I mention that you and I have worked on a similar project?"*

## Make yourself referable

If you want others to refer you and invest their resources in helping you, then you need to be prepared to make it easy for them. You also need to remember that anyone referring you is risking their reputation and relationships, so it is important you remove any potential risk.

Be very clear on how you can help and how the person you are being introduced to will benefit from your services. You need a clear **VALUE PROPOSITION (VP).**

> *"We have 20 years' experience working with professional services firms, helping them to be more effective at winning business. We work with groups of individuals to improve their skills, internal teams to embed those skills and management teams to ensure performance improvement and a measurable increase in new business is achieved".*

Find out about the goals and priorities of the people you want to meet, if you can. This way you can make your VP even more relevant and compelling.

*"I've heard that Flax is keen to help reduce the cost of their claims, I can help with this and provide some insights from a recent study".*

*"I know reducing operating costs is a priority for many companies in this sector and we have developed a piece of software to help companies manage their contracts and identify unnecessary costs".*

**Increasing "social debt"**

Increasing your social debt with clients and contacts will help to leverage value in terms of referrals and introductions. There are a number of ways to do this:

- Create value by helping clients with their client relationships;
- Provide information and intelligence;
- Provide referrals and introductions to them.

**Asking for referrals at the right time**

It is best to ask for a referral from a client just after you have completed a successful piece of work.

Alternatively, after you have made a presentation at a seminar or an individual client presentation. While they may not need your services, they know what value you can provide and may be happy to recommend you.

*"I realise that this is not anything you need right now, but having heard this presentation is there anyone you know who would benefit, that I should speak to?"*

**Measuring results**

Once you have set up your referral system and begun using it to build your pipeline, you need to monitor your progress and make sure you are getting a return on your investment and the results you want. Use the measures below to monitor your progress and manage your referral system.

- How many introductions and referrals are you getting per month/per quarter (whatever is a realistic time frame)?
- How many meetings are you getting from your introductions and referrals?
- What is the conversion rate to new business?
- Are the opportunities arising converting quicker?

**Summary of what you have learnt in this chapter**

- **Referrals must be a priority.** Rather than a supporting activity, referral selling must be a principle way of winning business and a part of your daily activity.
- **Be referable.** Be clear on what you offer clients and how you can help so that your referees will be more comfortable introducing you.
- **Don't rely on accidental referrals.** It is important to be clear on who you want to attract as clients and how your network can help you get referrals to those clients.
- **Develop your skills.** Never take referrals for granted as an "easy" win. Asking other people to provide you with value from their relationships takes care and skill.
- **Don't wait for the pipeline to dry up.** Put a sales referral process into place now to drive high-quality referrals consistently, so that you›re not left scrambling when the pipeline stops flowing.
- **Overcoming the fear of rejection is vital.** Be courageous and ask people with whom you have a good relationship to help you build your pipeline of business.
- **Make a plan and measure it.** Like any other business activity, you need a plan. Put the metrics in place to measure what you are doing, to ensure it is working and to identify areas of improvement if needs be.

# WIN IT

# Chapter 4

## How clients make decisions

Today's buyers of professional services are more educated than ever about what they need and the solutions available and will resist anything they perceive to be a "hard sell". They are not willing to spend time with professional advisers who are just there to talk about their capabilities and service offerings. Today's buyers want to spend time with advisers who can help them, provide an alternative perspective and who promote themselves as thought leaders and teachers.

In 2015, I worked in collaboration with Professor Chris Mckenna, who was then the director of the Centre for Professional Services at Said Business School. We looked at the models for sales and client development in law firms. During the study and in my conversations with buyers of legal services, I asked 2 questions, *"What is it that lawyers do that you really value?"* and *"What is it that you would like lawyers to do more of?"* Not surprisingly the answer was very similar and pretty much the same from all the buyers I spoke to and that was *"come to us with ideas and insight, share your experiences with us and tell us what we should be thinking about that we are not".*

This study focused on how lawyers engage with their clients, however it is my belief that this is one of the most effective ways you can create value for clients across the professional services sector.

It's simple, professional advisers who are successful sellers engage in client-centric conversations with clients. The ability to lead a highly client-centric conversation is one of the most significant differences between high performing sellers and core performers. This means focusing on the client's business, understanding and helping people explore their problems and addressing their priorities. Fundamentally selling is about helping your clients to succeed and to be better off as a result of working with you.

In this chapter, I will look at how individuals can engage successfully with a client's agenda; focus on the client's challenges and the items at the top of their agenda that they need to fix and collaborate effectively with clients to find solutions that will work.

A winning sales conversation means the seller has a clear goal and the ability to lead the conversation to deliver mutual value.

## How buyers make decisions

To connect with a client on their agenda and to talk about what is important to them, you need to understand and be able to influence their decisions.

The purchase of professional services is defined as a "complex decision" and buyers involved in influencing and making these decisions go through a number of very distinct phases, which we call "The Continuum of Decision-Making" or you might hear it referred to as "The Buyers Journey".

One of the distinguishing characteristics of individuals who are successful at selling high-value professional services is that they understand how buyers make complex decisions, they recognise where buyers are in their decision-making and they have the strategies and skills to influence buyers and the decisions they make.

The B2B buyers' survey 2019 found that sellers who engage early in their clients' and prospects' buying journey and who stay in touch throughout establish a material competitive advantage.

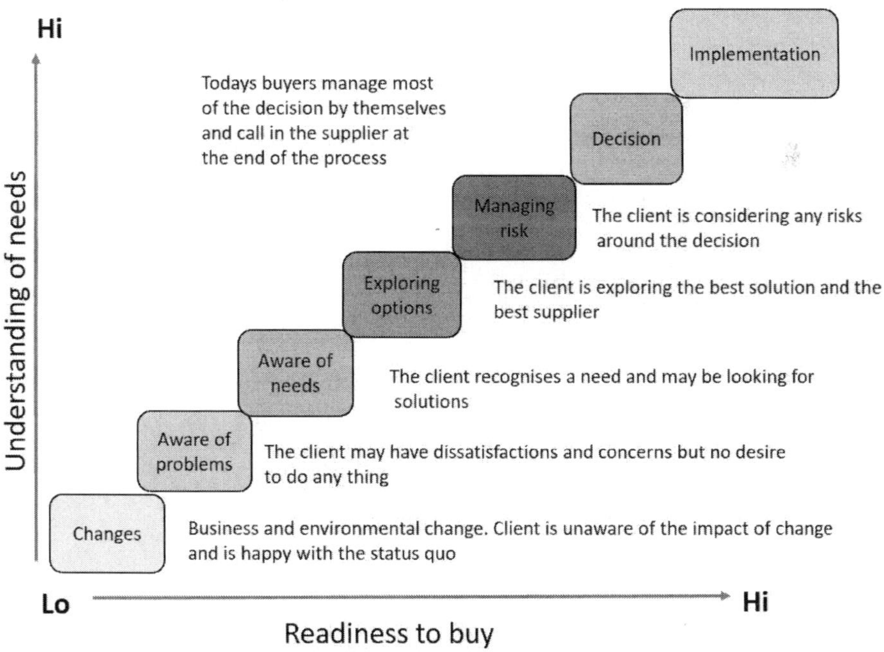


fig 6. Buyers journey

### Influencing the client at each stage of the decision-making continuum

**Changes –** Your client's needs arise as a direct result of change or failure. This may be in the client's business or in their external environment. They may be operating in a market where there is legislative or regulatory change on the horizon or significant technological change, or internally, there may be personnel changes or some kind of company reorganisation. However, while change or failure may trigger future requirements, many clients are unaware of the impact of change and are happy with the status quo, despite the change that is going on around them. This stage of the decision-making continuum is your best opportunity to create real value for clients and prospects. This is when you can shape your client's thinking, sell ideas and perspectives and provide insights that influence your client's agenda. The more you do at this stage to influence your client's thinking and shape their agenda, the stronger your competitive advantage will be. Furthermore this stage in clients' decision-making is when there is least competitive activity.

As I have already mentioned, research by the Corporate Executive Board identified that the ability to "educate" clients is a distinguishing characteristic of high performing sellers. This early stage is a great opportunity to educate.

See the table below which identifies what high performing sellers do differently at this stage in clients' decision-making and the common traps that you can fall into, which means you may miss vital opportunities.

| What high performing sellers do | What core performing sellers do | Common traps |
|---|---|---|
| Stay close. Proactive.<br><br>Stay abreast of market trends and market developments.<br><br>Promote themselves as a thought leader and shape the client's agenda.<br><br>Maintain social contact.<br><br>Seek referrals. | Focus on developed opportunities.<br><br>Don't actively engage with clients in between transactions.<br><br>Reactive. Wait for inbound enquiries. | Not proactive. Don't stay in touch with clients and prospects and miss opportunities.<br><br>Not close enough to clients' and prospects' business or market and miss changes. |

**Awareness of problems –** Most clients have a number of challenges to deal with. They may be concerned that they cannot comply with current regulations, or they may be unhappy with their current auditors; maybe the integration from a recent acquisition is not going well and they are not leveraging sufficient value. However, do not assume that if a client expresses these concerns that they are looking for a solution from you.

If the cost (financial, risk and disruption are all costs of change) of resolving these problems outweighs the client's perception of the value they will gain, they will stay put.

Status quo bias is one of the principle reasons why apparently promising sales opportunities end in "No Decision". If your client can't see sufficient contrast between their current situation and how much better off they could be, they are more likely to stick with what they know – because it's easier.

If you are going to persuade your client of the need for change, you need to start by helping them to recognise that the status quo is unsafe. You need to explore the threats, risks, and costs of staying put – the cost of inaction, and contrast that with the benefits and opportunities, if they changed.

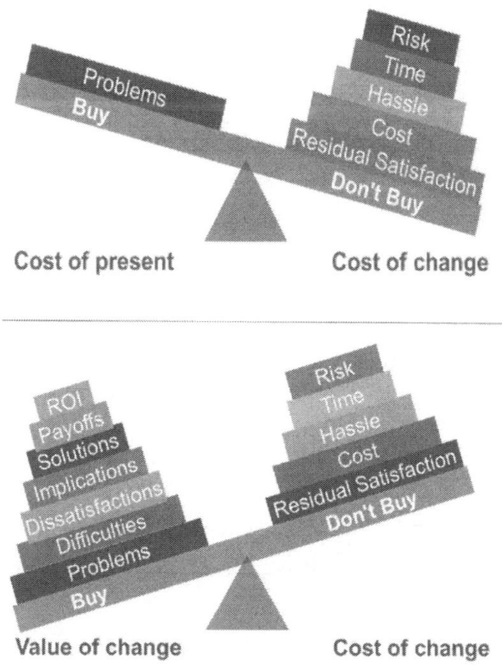


fig 7. Balance model

Selling the upside of your solution to clients that are living with problems will not be enough to persuade them to change. You will significantly improve your chances of success if you first explore with your client the dangers of staying put and then focus on the benefits of change.

The table below identifies what high performing sellers do differently at this stage in clients' decision-making and the common traps that you can fall into, which result in promising and attractive opportunities ending in "No Decision"

| What high performing sellers do | What core performing sellers do | Common traps |
|---|---|---|
| Stay in touch.<br>Proactively seek opportunities<br>Explores client's challenges, concerns and dissatisfactions.<br>Develop problems into needs.<br>Disrupt the status quo.<br>Use insights to educate clients.<br>Have client-centric conversations with clients. | Limited contact with existing clients.<br>Little or no contact with prospects.<br>Focus on developed opportunities.<br>Wait for inbound enquiries.<br>Have solution-centred conversations with clients. | Offer solutions too early and focus on the benefits the client can gain before the client recognises they can't continue with their status quo. |

**Awareness of needs –** At this stage, the client has recognised their needs and is looking for solutions. At this stage clients will often approach their advisers and present them with their needs in the form of solutions *" we need to look at directors agreements", "we need to look at refinancing the business", "we want to look at the business rates we pay on city centre properties".* It is very tempting to respond by offering solutions. However, it is important that you understand the underlying need, as it is possible the client's diagnosis of the required solution is wrong or incomplete. The chances are the client will be expecting some sort of proposal from you at this stage, which will, potentially, involve a significant amount of work. You should try to qualify the opportunity at this point. Find out who the other stakeholders are that have an interest. Assess competitor activity, which will be increasing now. See if you can find out why they want the solution they have asked for and what benefits are they looking to achieve? Most importantly, your solutions must be tailored to what the client says they want.

In my experience, working collaboratively with clients to develop the solution is a highly effective approach and one I would always use in preference to presenting the "finished article".

See the table below which identifies what high performing sellers do differently at this stage in clients' decision-making and the common traps that you can fall into.

| What high performing sellers do | What core performing sellers do | Common traps |
|---|---|---|
| Engage and influence clients in earlier stages.<br><br>If presented with needs in the form of solutions, take them back up their decision-making to understand underlying needs.<br><br>Willing to challenge if the solution requested seems wrong or incomplete.<br><br>Solutions tailored to client's needs.<br><br>Actively monitor competitor activity.<br><br>Qualify the decision-making process and stakeholders involved. | Reactive and respond to client's requests.<br><br>Focus on presenting solutions.<br><br>May be unaware of competitor activity. | Solutions may be incomplete or not sufficiently tailored to client's requirements. |

**Exploring options –** At some point in every high value, complex decision, the client will go out to the market to see who they might want to instruct. At this stage, the client is not thinking about "what they need" but "how they want to buy it".

This is when clients send out their RFP and run a tender – be it formal or informal, buyers of professional services will always compare potential suppliers before making a decision. That might well include internal teams, so don't forget them when you are monitoring competitor activity.

This is the stage when many professional advisers engage with clients for the first time, which really is too late. If you have not engaged in the earlier stages of the client's decision-making process and have not been actively influencing key stakeholders, your chances of success are slim.

This is the stage of the decision-making continuum when there is most competitor activity as clients are actively reviewing potential suppliers. At this stage in decision-making, clients will be considering their "Decision Criteria", which they will use to compare suppliers.

Your technical expertise is a given by this stage of clients' decision-making. Clients use other factors to compare suppliers, such as sector knowledge, geographical footprint, fees, the size of teams, and your technology and of course "do we like you?"

You need to know what decision criteria your clients will use to compare suppliers. You also need to understand their priorities – their "must have", their "nice to have" and be able to demonstrate your fit.

Incidentally, most sellers of professional services think the fee is the most important criteria in their choice of supplier. While fees are important, more often than not it is not the number one decision criterion.

In recent years, more and more professional services have, in the eyes of clients, been commoditised and this is where price is important. However, there are still many areas of professional expertise that clients expect to pay an appropriate fee for and where the fee is not the most important criterion.

I was running a client panel in Europe a while ago for a large city law firm. The then GC for a large electronics business in Europe was very clear. There were some services for which he didn't care who did the work, as long as they responded quickly, and it was done for a pre-agreed fixed fee. There were other services, such as corporate tax advice or regulatory advice that most firms could *"stick another nought on the invoice and we'd still pay it"*, because the consequences if it were to go wrong were significant and would have a serious impact on the business.

So, I always advise people, when thinking about the appropriate fee to charge to ask:

*"What is the consequence for the business if this was to go wrong?"* and *"What are the benefits to the client if they address this and make it a priority?"*

See the table below which identifies what high performing sellers do differently at this stage in clients' decision-making and the common traps that you can fall into, which means you lose out to competitors.

| What high performing sellers do | What core performing sellers do | Common traps |
|---|---|---|
| Engage early in clients' decision-making to influence clients' needs & decision criteria to establish competitor advantage. | Bid for everything | Engage too late. |
| Engage early with key stakeholders and understand decision-making. | Engage late in the clients' decision-making | Take too much at face value. |
| Monitor competitor activity. | Take any needs the client presents at face value. | Limited number of stakeholder contacts. |
| Make conscious bid-no bid decisions, if necessary. | Take information on decision-making at face value. | Make assumptions about decision criteria. |
| Create client-centric proposals and presentations which may be worked on in collaboration with the client. | Proposals and presentations are seller and solution centric. | |
| | Ignore competitor activity | |

**Managing risk** – At some stage in every high value complex decision the client will consider any potential risks in relation to the impending decision. These may be specific concerns such as *"we've not used these people before for this type of work"*, or vague worries *"is this going to be very disruptive?" "Are we sure we are set up to get the value from this?" "will we be able to implement this effectively?"*

The client may not volunteer these concerns, however, unresolved concerns, particularly around risk and value are another reason why apparently promising opportunities result in "No Decision" – *"we liked what we saw but it's just too risky so let's stay put and look at it again in 12 months".*

You need to uncover any concerns that clients and prospects may have. Your-day to-day contacts may have no worries, but there may be others elsewhere in the stakeholder network who don't know you so well, who may be worried about something and you need to know. Pre-empting and dealing with concerns can be the difference between winning and losing the sale. Using testimonials and references to reduce perceived risks is highly effective at this stage.

The common pitfall is that sellers dismiss any concerns or try to address them by continuing to reinforce the benefits of their solution.

**Implementation** – At this stage you and your colleagues are actively involved in service delivery. If it is a new piece of work, then it is important to stay close to the client, even if you are not delivering what you have sold. You need to stay visible to ensure everything goes smoothly. Minor difficulties can arise at this stage, which may become major concerns if not dealt with immediately. From a sales perspective, implementation is often a missed opportunity. During implementation, you and your colleagues have more access to clients than at any other time and more access to the wider business. Use this time to identify other opportunities and get to know other key stakeholders. This is also a good time to build your knowledge of competitors.

In chapter 13, I will be looking at on-boarding new clients to maximise the value and sustainability of relationships.

See the table below which identifies what high performing sellers do differently at this stage in clients' decision-making and the common traps that you can fall into, which means you miss opportunities.

| What high performing sellers do | What core performing sellers do | Common traps |
|---|---|---|
| Stay close to the client.<br><br>Proactively look for further sales opportunities.<br><br>Promote success.<br><br>Seek referrals externally and internally to other stakeholders.<br><br>Stay close to colleagues in the implementation team. | Focus on service delivery and miss other opportunities.<br><br>Move onto the next sales opportunity. | The person who has sold the service doesn't stay in touch with the client. Not enough communication internally about the client's expectations leading to dissatisfaction. |

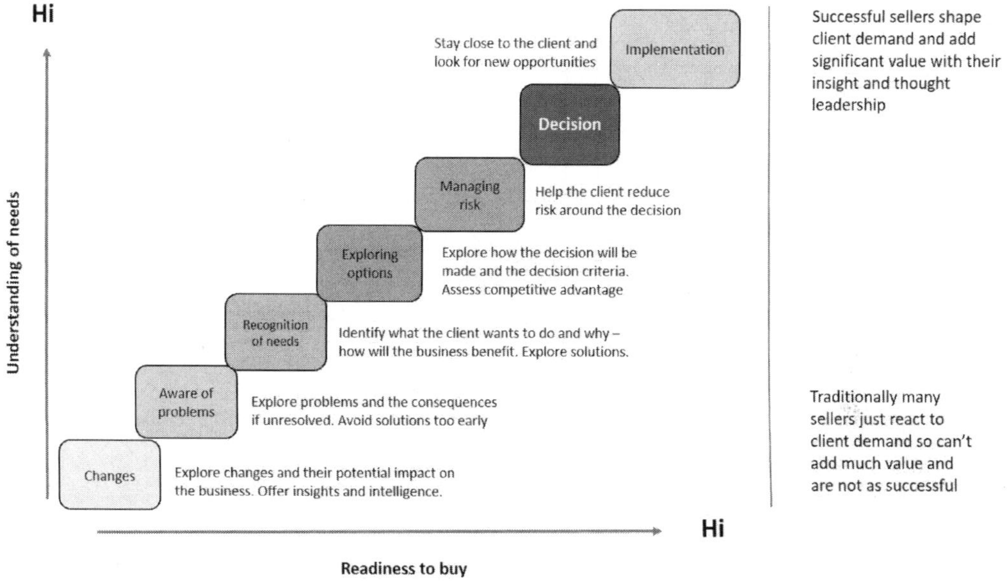


fig 8. The Buyers Journey - strategies

**A case in point...**

In our company, we had used the same firm of accountants for a number of years. They were local, understood our business and we got on well with the partner who looked after our business. Then one day, he told us he was retiring **[changes]** and would like to introduce the person he wanted to recommend to take over our account. We knew that at some point the partner we had worked with in recent years would want to retire, it wasn't a shock.

The following week we met the person who would be taking over. I liked her and found her pleasant to deal with but I was concerned **[awareness of problems]** that she didn't really understand a business such as ours and I thought she asked questions for which, I felt, she should have known the answers. Furthermore, she wasn't based in the local office. Nevertheless, at this point we felt there was no need to change accountants. Over the next few months we had a bit of difficulty with her not being based locally but still felt no great desire to find new accountants. Then, in the January she forgot to file our tax return on time, and we were fined. So, we had reached a tipping point. We decided we could no longer stick with the accountants we had used for so many years and that we needed a new firm. **[Awareness of needs]** Before we went to meet any new accountants, we sat down and decided what we wanted **[exploring options]** and agreed we needed a local firm, a firm that was familiar with small businesses, not wildly expensive and with a team of people we wanted to work with. We met three firms and eventually selected the firm we wanted to instruct. But before we went ahead, we asked ourselves *"Is this the right decision?", "are we throwing out the baby with the bath water?", "it was only one mistake – are we overreacting?"* **[managing risk]**.We then went ahead and instructed our new accountants. They on-boarded us successfully and all went well. **[Implementation]**

**Understanding clients' decision criteria**

Earlier in this chapter, I talked about influencing clients in **Exploring Options**. At this stage of their decision-making, clients' attention moves from "what do we need?" to "how do we want to buy it?" So, clients consider their **Decision Criteria (DC)**. Here are a few facts about decision criteria that will help you influence clients during the Exploring Options phase of decision-making.

fig 9. Decision criteria

- Your technical expertise is taken as given by the time clients reach this stage of their decision-making, so clients' decision criteria focus on factors such as how you engage with them, how you manage service delivery etc. As I mentioned in previously, this could include sector expertise, the management information you provide, certainty around fees, location of offices, the size of your team, responsiveness and added value services.

- Decision criteria will have different priorities – some will be "must haves" (we call these crucial) and some will be "nice to haves" (we call these incidental).
- Clients use decision criteria to compare competing suppliers. Whatever the format of the pitch, and however formal or informal, there will always be competition. Ensuring that you "match" the client's decision criteria and match them better than competitors is key to establishing competitive advantage.
- Your client may express their criteria in a vague or "soft" way. A common trap is to make assumptions. This is very common in the case of "added value services". Added value services is a frequently used decision criterion, but clients may have different requirements, so it is important to explore what they mean by added value services.
- If you engage early with clients in their decision-making process, you can influence the criteria they use to select their advisers. By suggesting criteria where you are strong and building value for that, you can gain competitive advantage early in the decision-making.
- Decision criteria live on! Not only are they used by clients to compare suppliers during the sales process, clients also use them to evaluate suppliers after you have been appointed and once you are doing the work.

- Remember there may be a number of people involved in making, influencing and scrutinising decisions. Each of these people may have different criteria and almost certainly, different priorities. For example, the priority for client contacts you work with day-to-day will be "do we like them and can we work with them?". If procurement is involved, fees and how they can manage supplier performance (management information) will be a priority.

**A case in point ...**

The market for training and consultancy is very crowded, with lots of suppliers providing similar services. However, few have the operational sales experience that I do (for a number of years I had targets to meet and a payroll of six consultants I had to feed, so sales effectiveness was pretty important). Whenever possible, I introduce operational sales experience as a decision criterion and build the value around having "done the job". By doing this I can build competitive advantage in what is an oversupplied market.

**There are a number of questions you can use to establish clients' decision criteria and their relative importance – here are some suggestions.**

*"What is it you're looking for from the firm that you appoint for this?"*

*"How will you choose the supplier for this?"*

*"What's most important?"*

*"What's important to the other people involved in choosing suppliers?"*

*"Why did you choose your current advisers?"*

*"Is there anything your current advisers don't do that you would like them to?"*

*"How important is x, when selecting suppliers?"*

*"A number of people we work with tell us y is important, is it important for you?"*

*"What do you like best about the firms you use for ....?"*

## Using decision criteria to build competitive advantage

Understanding your competition and developing successful strategies to manage competitors begins with understanding where your competition may come from. There are five sources of competition:

| **Sources of competition**<br>**Direct competition** | there are no dominant suppliers i.e. you might have an equal standing with others and you are all competing for the same business |
|---|---|
| **Competitors account** | one of your competitors is the established supplier |
| **Your account** | you are the established supplier |
| **Internal competition** | where individuals or departments believe they can provide what you do |
| **Competition for funds** | where there is no specific budget for what you do and so there is a risk funds will be used for other purposes |

If you are in direct competition with other suppliers or one of your competitors is an established supplier, you need an accurate and objective understanding of your competitor's relationship with a client so that you can establish and strengthen your competitive advantage.

Clients use their decision criteria to compare competing suppliers during the sales process, so it is important to understand how they see you compared to your competitors, so that you can develop your "competitive selling strategies" to build and strengthen your competitive advantage.

## Competitive selling strategies

**Strength.**
In relation to crucial DCs, the client sees you as stronger than competitors. The strategy here is to seek to reinforce your strengths to build competitive advantage.

**Weakness**
The client sees you as weaker than competitors in relation to crucial DCs. The strategy here is to redefine the DC so that you can meet the client's underlying need or to build up the importance of other DCs.

**Opportunity**
The client sees you as strong in relation to DCs which are not important to them. The strategy here is to build up the importance of the DC where you are seen as strong in order to gain competitive advantage.

**Threat**
The client recognises competitors have strengths in relation to DCs that you don't – albeit in areas not important to them. Nevertheless, this is a potential risk and the strategy is to build up the importance of other DCs where you are strong.

**Summary of what you have learnt in this chapter**

1. **Clients and prospects go through a number of distinct phases when making high value purchasing decisions** – high performers recognise where clients are on the client decision continuum and use the appropriate strategies to influence clients.
2. **High performers engage early in decision-making when clients and prospects are undergoing change or failure.** They use insights and thought leadership to educate clients and prospects and shape their agenda.
3. **Avoid status quo bias** – high performers encourage clients and prospects to explore the risks of staying put and living with problems to avoid "No Decision".
4. **Tailor solutions to meet clients' needs** and work collaboratively with clients and prospects to design appropriate solutions.
5. **Ensure all proposals and presentations are client centric.** Avoiding anything that is too technical or solution centred.
6. **Get to know all the stakeholders who can make and influence decisions** – they navigate the stakeholder network to gain influence with key stakeholders in the decision.
7. **Deal with perceived risks.**
8. **Monitor competitor activity.**

# Chapter 5

## How to identify and develop client needs

One of the distinguishing characteristics of high performing sellers is that they understand how clients' needs develop and how they can influence this. Inexperienced and less-skilled sellers on the other hand are more likely to make assumptions about a client's needs or attempt to persuade them they have need by describing the features of their products and services. In this chapter, I want to describe how clients develop and what individuals can do to influence that.

Firstly, I want to make a distinction between how needs develop for low value goods and services and how they develop for high value goods and services. Let me illustrate this a little further.

I was in a stationery shop recently and saw, what I thought, was a really well-designed set of "noise reduction" earphones in a neat little case, for my smart phone. I listen to podcasts and music on my smartphone a lot, when I am travelling, so I thought these earphones would be useful. They were £15 and without a lot of thought, other than, "I like those", I bought them. However, in contrast to that, when I bought my new laptop, it took me nearly a year from considering what I needed until I made a decision.

One of the characteristics of high value sales is that needs are not instant, they develop slowly and sellers may find they are talking to buyers at any point in this process. Success in selling high value goods and services requires a highly developed set of skills to engage effectively with buyers and influence the development of their needs.

So why is the development of needs in relation to high value goods and services so much more complex?

| Needs in a small, low value sale | Needs in a complex, high value sale |
|---|---|
| • Doesn't require consultation with others – you can make the decision as it is just your need.<br>• There is often a strong emotional component (many small items remain unopened and never used☺).<br>• The emotional component does exist in high value sales but is often subdued by the rational component.<br>• If it turns out to be a mistake, the cost and other consequences are minimal. | • The development of needs is likely to require input, consultation and the influence of a number of people involves a number of other people.<br>• The needs are rarely the wishes of a single person.<br>• Needs will need a rational justification, even if there is some underlying emotional or irrational driver.<br>• The wrong decision is likely to have far reaching consequences, hence the time it takes for the needs to develop. |

### How needs develop

Clients' needs develop along a continuum from very weak to very strong and it is important to listen closely to what clients say to you so that you can respond in the most effective way.

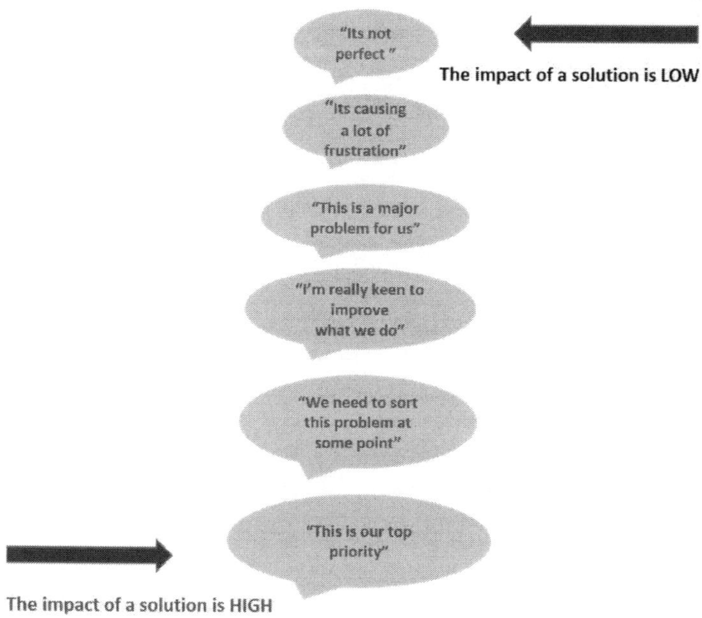


fig 10. Development of client needs

Let's look at this in a bit more detail.

My need for a new laptop began when I started to get frustrated with my existing laptop – some of the functionality wasn't great and it was a bit slow. However, if a laptop salesperson had approached me at this point, I would not have been interested. As time went on other problems arose and I became increasingly frustrated. Nevertheless, the laptop sales person would still have struggled to sell me a new computer. Then, I lost most of a white paper I was working on. The limitations of my existing laptop and the frustrations that I was living with translated into a desire for a solution – the time had come to change! If a laptop salesperson had called by at this point, I would have been very receptive to a solution.

What this illustrates is that clients' needs are expressed in two ways:

**Emerging needs –** These are statements of frustration and dissatisfaction

*"My current advisers are very slow", "I'm worried that we are not complying with current legislation", "We have a number of problems with supplier contracts". "The board is concerned that we are not leveraging the value we should from the recent acquisition".*

It is important to understand that clients live with problems. We refer to these problems as "emerging needs" because the client is not planning to take any action and is not looking for a solution.

On several occasions, when I have been mentoring fee earners to help them progress sales opportunities, individuals have presented me with a list of client problems, as indicators of likely success. Just because a client is willing to share their problems and frustrations with you, does not mean they are planning to take any action or are looking for a solution.

**Explicit needs** – These are statements of intent to take action.

*"We need to change our advisers", "We need to reduce our fees", and "The board's priority is to reduce our tax liability".*

At this stage the client wants to take action and is looking for a solution. Explicit needs are more accurate indicators of sales success than emerging needs.

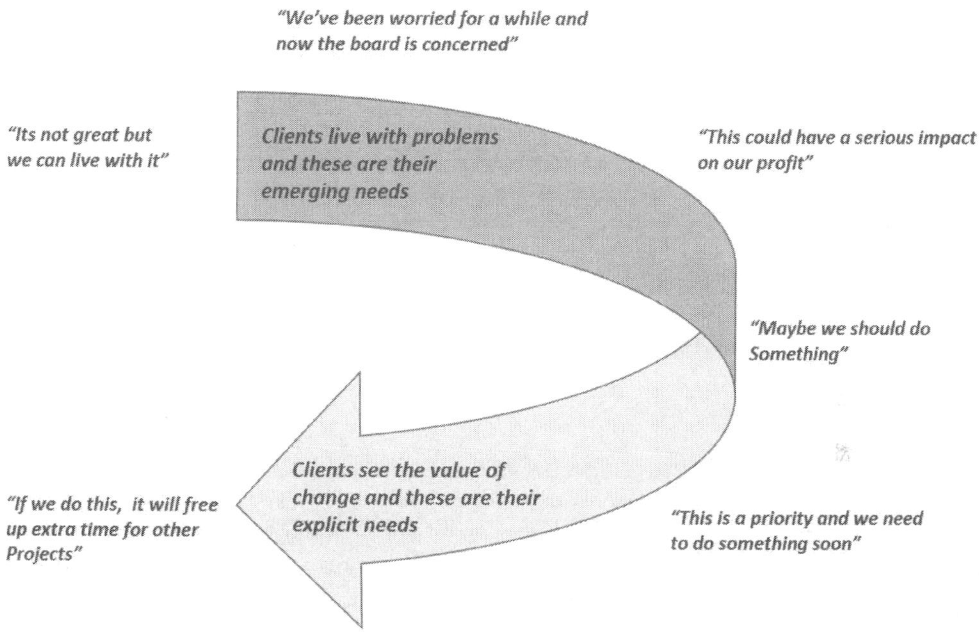


fig 11. How clients needs develop

### Responding to clients' needs

One of the characteristics of high value sales is:

- High performing sellers treat emerging needs and explicit needs differently;
- Less successful and inexperienced sellers don't differentiate between emerging needs and explicit needs and treat them in exactly the same way.

### Explicit needs

Most sellers feel comfortable dealing with clients' explicit needs. At this point in their decision-making, a client will have recognised they have a need for which they want a solution and will approach the seller because they are ready to begin exploring solutions.

Clients will often present their needs as solutions they want advisers to deliver. However, it is possible the client's diagnosis of the required solution is wrong or incomplete, so you need to take the client back up their decision-making process to check if the solution they are asking for is the best one.

*"Clients are inherently unreliable" – Hank Williams, Learning Curve*

Here's an example:

I was asked by a client on one occasion for some client care training for their legal support staff. I was a little bit concerned as the team was experienced and were long-standing members of staff. My initial response was "yes, we can do that". I then went on to ask if I could get some more information to understand the request a bit further. I explored, with the client, what they wanted to achieve, what had changed and whether there was anything specific that they were worried about. It turned out there had been some significant reorganisation. Legal secretaries who had previously been attached to a specific department were now in a central services group. Consequently, they felt detached from the business and less involved than previously. They felt undervalued and were demotivated and as a consequence, standards of client engagement and service delivery had deteriorated.

What this conversation with the client revealed was that the underlying problem was due to a lack of communication for which client care training was not the solution. The client went back to the business and worked with an internal team on a programme on internal communication.

**Emerging needs**

These are more difficult to respond to successfully, but if you can gain influence with clients at this stage of their decision-making, you will gain considerable competitive advantage.

As I explained earlier, clients live with problems. Any client making a high value purchasing decision must balance two opposing factors – the seriousness of the problem and the cost of the solution.

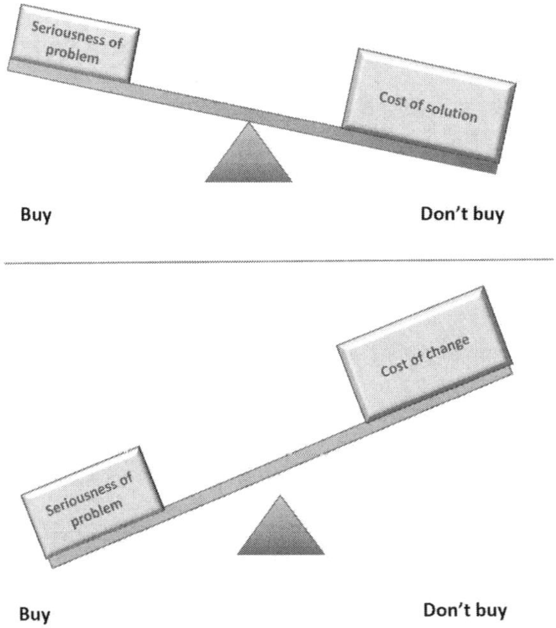


fig 12 Cost vs Change

If the cost of the solution outweighs the client's perception of the seriousness of the problem, they will stay put and continue to live with the problem. Reducing the cost of the solution is neither effective, nor commercially sensible, as the only thing that will suffer is your profitability.

The other reason clients live with problems is a phenomenon called **Status Quo Bias** and if a seller can disengage a buyer – and others involved in the decision – from their status quo bias, they are more likely to convert opportunities into successful sales outcomes.

Status quo bias is a client's preference for their current situation. I work with many fee earners who are frustrated by their clients' and prospects' willingness to live with, what may be, quite significant and complex problems. The environment for most businesses is more challenging than ever. Business leaders are operating with more change and uncertainty than in the past and so more often than not, the status quo, however imperfect it might be, will seem a more attractive option than taking action.

Buyer behaviour is changing too which is increasing the likelihood of status quo bias.

**Stakeholders are increasing –** Buying decisions involve an increasing number of stakeholders. Each stakeholder may be at a different point in their decision-making and will have different priorities. More people and more competing priorities mean there is a greater chance that sales opportunities will stall and or stop. Just one doubting voice in a buying team is enough to unravel an otherwise attractive and certain sale and result in a decision to *"stay put for now".*

**Rising scepticism –** Ever since the recession in 2008, business leaders have been more sceptical and risk averse. Buyers have a tendency to trust what they know, even though what they know might be less than perfect – in other words, buyers would rather stick with the status quo than risk doing something different. In any high value decision, buyers are more interested in avoiding a loss than experiencing an equivalent gain.

Status quo bias is also known as "the cost of change". If the cost of change outweighs the value clients perceive they will get they will stay put?

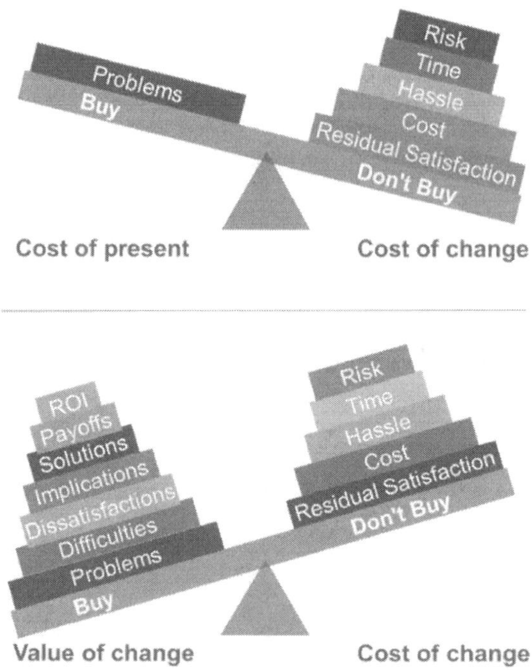


fig 13. Balance model

## Overcoming status quo bias and winning business

There are a number of strategies that sellers of professional services can use to overcome status quo bias. Before we look at these in detail, let me highlight a common pitfall that sellers fall into when faced with status quo bias. The temptation is to present all the benefits a buyer can gain by taking action. Buyers, however, are more concerned about the loss they might suffer if they were to act, rather than the gain they may obtain. The temptation is to unload the cost side of the balance. However, because there is a tendency to stay with what we know, the reasons to justify that decision are well thought through.

*"We know our current advisers are a bit slow and there have been a few changes in the team but they do know us".*

*"We go back a long way and it's going to take the team a long time to bring you up to speed".*

*"It's not great but they do know us – warts and all".*

What is less well thought through, is the cost of doing nothing, the risks of continuing to live with the current situation.

So the more effective strategy for dealing with emerging needs and disengaging a client from their status quo bias is to focus on the problem the client is living with and encourage them to think about the size and the extent of the problem and the consequences of not taking action.

**Summary of what you have learnt in this chapter**

- **Clients' needs develop along a continuum from very weak to very strong;**
- **There are broadly two categories of client needs;**
- **Emerging needs** – are expressed as problems and dissatisfactions which clients are happy to live with;
- **Explicit needs –** are expressed as a desire or intent to take action and you can begin to explore problems;
- **Emerging needs can be developed** – by encouraging the client to recognise the consequence of continuing to live with problems. This will increase their perception of the seriousness of the problem.

# Chapter 6

## Leading a winning sales conversation

*"Stop selling, start helping" – Zig Ziglar*

Today's buyers of professional services are more educated than ever about what they need and the solutions available. As such they will resist anything they perceive to be a "hard sell". They are not willing to spend time with professional advisers who are just there to talk about their capabilities and service offerings. Today's buyers want to spend time with advisers who listen to them, understand their needs, shape their thinking, provide an alternative perspective and who promote themselves as thought leaders and teachers.

Inexperienced sellers believe they have to show and tell. Persistent pitching and presentations of credentials, which are of no interest or relevance, will leave the buyer feeling irritated and the seller feeling pushy and uncomfortable. A telling style of selling is not the basis of an effective sales conversation.

The single most important sales behaviour is asking questions and having a good questioning strategy. High performing sellers spend significantly more time asking questions than giving information and solutions, compared to core performers.

Fundamentally, selling is about helping your clients to succeed and be better off as a result of working with you. For this you need a good questioning strategy.

Interestingly, when buyers were asked what influenced their choice of supplier, they said, "They listened to me" and "They understood my needs". Neither of these can be achieved if you don't focus on the client and ask questions.

In this chapter I will look at why questions are important and how to develop an effective questioning strategy.

*"Seek to be interested not interesting" – Stephen Covey*

**Why are questions important?**

Questions help you to find out what's going on in your clients' or prospects' world. At a relationship level, they help you connect with your clients and prospects, to get to know them personally and to build rapport. As well as building rapport, good questions help you to establish your credibility and demonstrate integrity, which helps to build the trust that underpins a great sales conversation.

At a task level, questions help you to understand the client's agenda and what is important to them and enable you to gather all the key information you need to identify and progress sales opportunities. Questions encourage the client to do their own thinking about their problems and needs, and they help to disrupt and reshape their thoughts. Questions are the most powerful behaviour in persuading others to change their thoughts and actions, helping you to drive sales forward and win business.

Finally, questions put you in the driving seat. Questions enable you to lead the conversation and to control the flow of information.

A quick word of warning before we move on to look at questions in more detail. The emphasis is on good questions, which essentially help the client. You need to avoid questions for which you should already have the answers or have found out the information elsewhere, such as the company website. For example:

*"How many employees do you have"?* Or *"where is your head office?"*

Questions such as these are of no value to the client and will irritate them. These questions are counterproductive in terms of your relationship with the client and you will very quickly lose the interest of the client and your credibility. If you need to check if your information is correct, then phrase the question differently.

*"I see on your website that you currently have 200 staff. Is that likely to increase or decrease?"*

### Your questioning framework

If you want to be effective at building relationships and identifying and developing new business opportunities, you need an effective questioning framework. You need to focus on:

- Questions to build and reinforce rapport;
- Questions to uncover and explore problems – these are your client's EMERGING needs;
- Questions to uncover and explore needs – these are your client's priorities for action;
- Questions to uncover and influence decision criteria;
- Questions to understand who makes, influences and scrutinises decisions;
- Questions to learn about competitors.

Huthwaite Research Group discovered that one of the distinguishing behaviours of high performing sellers is questions. They ask questions in a ratio of at least 3.5:1 giving clients information and they have a well-planned questioning framework focused on the key information needed to develop new business opportunities.

**Questions to build and reinforce rapport**

These questions are useful at the outset of a sales conversation as they help you to connect personally with your client. A word of warning, however – rapport building questions that seem superficial and do not sound genuine will not be effective. If you know your client well your questions will be more authentic, so frame them around what you know.

*"Last time we spoke you were just about to go away – how was your holiday"?*

*"Wasn't it lovely weather last weekend, did you get any golf in"?*

*"How's your son, I remember he wasn't well when we met last month"?*

If you are going to be exploring, what might be sensitive issues with a client, or challenging their current perspective on something, you need to have established a good level of rapport.

Some people don't want to engage in "small talk", they just want to concentrate on business, in which case these rapport building questions and chit-chat at the beginning of a conversation may not be appropriate.

**Questions to uncover and explore problems – Your client or prospect's emerging needs**

In chapter 5 we highlighted the fact that clients live with problems and that if the cost of change outweighs the value of change, they will stay put. We call this "status quo bias".

These are called **problem-centred** questions and they help you to uncover the **EXISTENCE**, **SIZE** and **IMPACT** of a problem. Encouraging your client or prospect to think about their problems in this way, will help them to recognise the seriousness of the problem and the need to resolve it.

| | |
|---|---|
| **Adviser** | *Kerry, how did the recent property portfolio acquisition go – it was a big one for you I seem to remember?* |
| **Client** | *Yes, it was a substantial deal and it went well thanks, you know the usual teething problems but nothing we wouldn't expect really.* |
| **Adviser** | *Oh, what teething problems?* |
| **Client** | *Well we are much slower integrating the new portfolio than we had hoped.* |
| **Adviser** | *Oh dear, why is that, what's happened since you did the acquisition?* |
| **Client** | *All sorts, you know how it is. I just don't think we are as good at project management as we think we are.* |
| **Adviser** | *Is it just poor project management or have you had other obstacles?* |
| **Client** | *Well we've lost a couple of members of the project team, so our resources are stretched, which isn't great.* |
| **Adviser** | *So is your lack of project management capability and lack of resources a view that is widely shared with your colleagues?* |
| **Client** | *Yes, it's certainly been discussed at the exec board.* |
| **Adviser** | *Where have you seen the greatest impact of this?* |
| **Client** | *We should be seeing significant economies of scale and I don't think we are.* |
| **Adviser** | *Is that having a significant impact on your bottom line?* |
| **Client** | *It must be ...........* |

**Further examples of problem-centred questions.**

As you become more experienced and confident in asking these questions, you will find there are certain highly effective questions that you can use in most sales conversations.

**Questions that help to identify the existence of a problem**

| *"What are the main challenges that you have at the moment?"*<br>*"What's stopping you reaching your goals"?*<br>*"What isn't' working very well for you at the moment"?*<br>*"Have you done anything about these problems?"* |
|---|

These are really high-level questions that will begin to encourage the client or prospect to concentrate on their current problems, difficulties and frustrations.

*"I was talking to one of my retail clients the other day and they are quite concerned about x which is affecting your sector – is this something you are concerned about?"*

*"I was at an energy briefing event last week. We heard about some interesting changes which I know some business are already concerned about. Is this something you are concerned about too?"*

*"How are you coping with the current market conditions?"*

*"How are you affected by the increase in competition"?*

Phrasing questions like this is a great way to demonstrate expertise, industry knowledge and will help to build your credibility. It also helps the buyer to think about challenges they may not have previously thought about.

*"You mentioned last time that you were undertaking a major strategic review of the business. What problems has that thrown up for you?"*

This is a more specific and focused question and demonstrates a good knowledge of the client or prospect's business. The more focused you can make your questions, the greater their impact will be.

**Questions to help to identify the size of the problem**

These questions are highly effective in beginning to "grow" the problem in the client's mind. One of the pitfalls that less-experienced and less-confident sellers fall into is, "let's find-out-what's-wrong-and-fix-it". Having uncovered the client or prospect's problem, they leap into presenting solutions and ideas to fix it. However, simply uncovering a problem does not mean the client or prospect wants a solution. These questions enable you to dig deeper to help your client or prospect to understand the seriousness of the problem.

*"Why is that a problem"?*

*"Who else is worried about that"?*

*"How long has that been worrying you"?*

Simple phrasing but highly effective!

**Questions to identify the impact of a problem**

These are highly effective questions for growing a problem in the mind of the client or prospect. These questions help the client or prospect to think about the impact and consequences of continuing to live with problems. These questions are extremely powerful in shifting the client or prospect away from their status quo and encouraging them to think about change. A client will not be interested in change or any sort of solution until they recognise their current situation is no longer an option.

*"If you don't fix this problem, what will the long-term consequences be"?*

*"What is it stopping you doing this?"*

*"How's that affecting the business"?*

*"How much time are you losing?"*

*"Is it restricting other activities?"*

*"Is it distracting the board"?*

*"What can't you do because you are tied up with all these other problems"?*

*"Is it damaging the company's reputation"?*

*"Is this having an effect on your relationship with your customers"?*

*"What's the effect on employee morale?"*

*"What's the impact on the bottom line?"*

There is no prescribed wording for problem-centred questions; it is important to vary the way in which you phrase your questions. The key to asking effective questions is to be clear in your mind of the purpose of the question and what you need to find out.

Here are some key words/phrases to help you explore your client's or prospect's problems

| | | |
|---|---|---|
| Awkward | Obstacles | Unhappy with |
| Difficult | Not going well | Not as effective as you would like |
| Restrictions | Concerns | Not fit for purpose |
| Constraints | Not ideal | Not performing as required |
| Frustrations | Anxious about | Not as easy as you would like |
| Worried | Uncomfortable with | |

**Questions to uncover and develop needs**

Problems are your client's and prospect's emerging needs, but at this point the client or prospect may not intend to do anything to resolve them. You need to ask more questions to explore problems further and develop them into explicit needs. The client is more likely to be interested and receptive to your ideas and solutions.

These are called **Value-centred questions** and they encourage the client to focus on positives. They help you to uncover the **EXISTENCE**, **IMPORTANCE** and **VALUE** of client needs. Value-centred questions help the client to recognise the value of resolving their problems and how much better off they could be – in other words the payoff of change.

Living with the status quo, however flawed that might be, is frequently easier for your client or prospect – it's often a case of "better the devil you know". If you can help your client or prospect to see that the future could be so much better, they are more likely to change.

The questions below can help you to do this.

| | |
|---|---|
| **Adviser** | *Belle, it's lovely to see you again. You have had a busy few months I guess since you joined.* |
| **Client** | *You could say that, but I have a much clearer picture now of how the land the lies!* |
| **Adviser** | *That's good! Last time we met you were quite concerned about the lack of management information and whether the business was controlling costs.* |
| **Adviser** | *Do you have a sense of what your main priorities are for the next 12–24 months?* |
| **Client** | *Oh, there are loads, there is so much to do to turn this business around and hit the profit targets. One thing I do need to get on with is controlling estate management costs.* |
| **Adviser** | *Is that not something the management team are working on?* |
| **Client** | *Yes, but there are a lot of conflicting time demands on them?* |
| **Adviser** | *So how would some additional resources allocated to controlling estate costs, improve profitability?* |
| **Client** | *Mmm, yes. We'd see some pretty quick results I think.* |
| **Adviser** | *Would that help you to move onto address some of the other priorities?* |
| **Client** | *Definitely.* |
| **Adviser** | *Where do you think you could have the greatest impact if extra resources were available for managing the estate costs* |
| **Client** | *That's a good question, probably some more acquisitions which we need to hit our growth target.* |
| **Adviser** | *Is that a priority for the board too?* |
| **Client** | *Our acquisition programme is a key to our growth, so yes ...* |

## Further examples of value-centred questions

As you become more experienced and confident in asking these questions, you will find there are certain highly effective questions that you can use in most sales conversations.

### Questions that help you identify the existence of a need

These are high-level questions. They are particularly useful if you have been encouraging a client to explore their problems and you want to encourage them to look forward and think about resolving their problems.

These questions are also useful for identifying any immediate needs and priorities a client or prospect has when you are talking to them.

*"Is this something you want to address?"*

*"What are your priorities?"*

*"Do you want to do something about this?"*

*"What do you think needs to happen to improve profitability?"*

The phrasing of these questions is very general:

*"Because of all the new regulation x has recently introduced a new system for monitoring the environment, is that something you are thinking about?"*

*"A lot of companies in your sector are changing their procedure for x, is that your intention too?"*

*"How have your requirements for x changed?"*

These questions are more specific. They demonstrate your knowledge and experience and help to build your credibility with the client. Questions which reference what other companies are doing are particularly effective in influencing clients and prospects – It's a case of *"Well if they are doing that we should too"*

### Questions that establish the importance of a need

These questions encourage your client to think about the value they would gain if they were to address their need. The more focused they are, the greater their impact on your client or prospect.

*"How will profitability increase if you were to address this?"*

*"Would availability of more resources improve employee commitment and productivity?"*

*"How much time could you save if that process was improved?"*

### Questions to identify the payoff

These questions dig a bit further and in doing so, they encourage the client to explore how else they would benefit by addressing their need and to recognise how much better off they could be. These questions build the client or prospect's desire to change and their interest in your solution.

*"If you were able to save all that time, what else could you do?"*

*"Have you had any thoughts on what you want to do?"*

*"I know you have a number of projects on hold, so if you could reduce costs by as much as you say, which projects could you then invest in?"*

*"If you increased your resource what else would it enable you to do?"*

*"You mentioned some time ago that you wanted to spend more time with clients, so with all this extra time you could have, will you be able to do that?"*

*"If you speed up the process by that much what else could your team do?"*

### Using questions to understand your clients' and prospects' underlying needs and problems

There will be many occasions when your clients or prospects will present their needs in the form of solutions which they want you to deliver.

*"We need an update on the latest tax changes".*

*"We need all our employment contracts reviewed".*

*"We want to update our performance management system".*

*"All our legal support staff should have client care training".*

Problem-centred and value-centred questions will help you to explore the underlying problems and needs to ensure your solution is both correct and complete.

*We need to review our employment contracts.*

*OK, We can do that for you. Can I just ask you a couple of questions to help me understand the background?*

*Why have you chosen to do this, now?*

*Why do you want to review your contracts?*

*What do you specifically need to improve?*

*Has something gone wrong that makes you think you need to change them?*

*Is there something specific that you are worried about?*

**Questions to uncover and influence decision criteria**

We talked about Decision Criteria, why they are important and how clients use them, in chapter 4. These questions help you to understand how a client or prospect will compare and select their suppliers. It will also enable you to understand their priorities – their "nice to haves" and their "musts haves". Decision Criteria are also the basis of competitive advantage. If, for example, the client sees you as very strong and stronger than competitors, in their most important DC, you will potentially have a competitive advantage. For example, if a client tells you that sector expertise is their number one decision criterion and they see you as the strongest in this area, then that is where you have a potential advantage over competitors. Likewise, if you are seen as weaker than competitors in DC that are important to your client, you need to know so that you can address it. So, these are important questions to ask your clients and prospects.

*"How will you select the firm you want to instruct for this?"*

*"When you select professional advisers, what is the most important thing you look for?"*

*"What are the top 3 things you look for from a professional firm?"*

*"Is there anything that would make you decide not to instruct a firm?"*

*"What about your colleagues, what is important for them in choosing a professional firm?"*

There may be specific areas where you are strong, and you can use your questions to influence their priorities and build your competitive advantage.

*"How important is sector knowledge for you in your choice of professional firms?"*

*"An increasing number of clients say that a firm's management information is their number 1 priority – how important is that for you?"*

There may be areas that are important to the client, but where they believe competitors are stronger. Questions may help you to reduce the importance of this decision criterion and reduce your competitor's advantage.

*"Some clients want partners to lead on work, which can be expensive for you. We tend to use partners to supervise work and more junior fee earners do the work, which is more cost effective. Is partner-led work important?"*

### Questions to find out about decision-makers

In chapter 4 we talked about the complexity of decision-making and how many more people are involved in B2B decisions than previously, so this part of your questioning framework is particularly important. Here are some examples of questions and no doubt there will be others that you will want to add to these.

*"Who else is involved in making this decision?"*

*"Is there anyone else that we haven't met yet, involved?"*

*"Who might say no?"*

*"How much scrutiny of decisions do you get from the board?"*

*"Is there anyone else you need to consult with on this?"*

*"Whose buy-in do we need for this project?"*

### Questions about competitors

This is always a difficult area and one that many inexperienced and less-confident sellers shy away from, however, it is highly unlikely that your clients and prospects will only be talking to you. However informal the sales process might appear, your competitors will be in the frame, even if you clients don't volunteer this. I have worked with fee earners on more than one sales opportunity and been told "they are not speaking to anyone else" only to then lose the job to another firm. Always assume there are always competitors in the frame (and they may be an in-house team) and don't expect clients to volunteer who else they are talking to. These questions are therefore very important to find out which of your competitors your client or prospect is talking to. You also need to know how the clients see the relative strengths and weaknesses of each of the firms they are talking to.

Your clients and prospects may well not want to share this information with you, but if you don't ask, you won't know – I don't want to tell you that? They certainly won't think any the worse of you for asking.

*"Are you talking to anyone else?"*

*"Who else are you talking to?"*

*"Have you got a firm you already use?"*

*"Who have you used in the past?"*

*"Do your colleagues have any preferred suppliers?"*

*"What do you see are our particular strengths?"*

*"What are the principle strengths of competitors?"*

*"Is there anything that puts us at a disadvantage?"*

| Question type | Purpose of the question | Example |
|---|---|---|
| Questions to establish and reinforce rapport | Useful at the start of a sales conversation to connect and establish rapport with your clients and prospects | *"Did you have a good journey?"*<br>*"How was your holiday"*<br>*"Did you manage to get to see the football last week – I know you were keen to get there if you could?"*<br>*"Did you enjoy the new wildlife film?"* |
| Questions to uncover the existence, size and impact of a problem | Use problem-centred questions to uncover and develop problems and grow their seriousness in the mind of the client or prospect. PC-Qs encourage the client to do their own thinking | *"What are the principle things you are concerned about?"*<br>*"Who else is worried about this?"*<br>*"How long has this been a problem?"*<br>*"How is it affecting other parts of the business?"*<br>*"If it's not resolved what will the longer-term impact be?"* |
| Questions to develop needs and payoff if the problem is resolved | Use value-centred questions to explore your clients' and prospects' needs and the value they would get if they addressed their needs. VC-Qs encourage the client to think about their needs and priorities and the payoff they could achieve | *"What do you plan to do about this?"*<br>*"Is it a priority?"*<br>*"Is improving your billing system a priority for you?"*<br>*"How much would cash flow improve if you improved your billing system?"*<br>*"How much management time could you save?"*<br>*"If you were able to improve cash flow what else could you do?"*<br>*"What other projects could you do if you saved all this time?"* |

| Question type | Purpose of the question | Example |
|---|---|---|
| Questions about decision-makers | These questions help to find out about who is involved in decision-making and their role and influence | *"Who else is involved?"*<br>*"Is there anyone else you need to consult?"*<br>*"How far up the organisation does approval for this project need to go?"*<br>*"Who has what role in decisions?"*<br>*"Is there anyone who might say no?"* |
| Questions about decision criteria | These questions help to find out how the client or prospect will evaluate and compare suppliers and can be used to influence criteria to strengthen competitive advantage | *"What criteria do you use to select firms"*<br>*"What is the most important thing you look for in a firm?"*<br>*"How important is X?"*<br>*"What are the top 3 things that influence your choice of firm?"* |
| Questions about competitors | These questions help to find out about competitors. They can also help to assess the relative strengths and weakness of competing firms | *"Who else are you speaking to?"*<br>*"Do you have a firm you use for this or have used in the past?"*<br>*"What do you like about x?"*<br>*"Where do you see our strengths lie?"*<br>*"Is there any reason why you or others would not want to instruct us?"* |

## Summary of the sales questioning framework

### Verbal listening skills

Throughout this chapter, we have concentrated on how to develop an effective questioning framework. However, as well as asking good questions you need to develop good listening as well:

*"Listen with the intent to understand, not with the intent to reply"*
*– Stephen Covey*

Using good verbal listening skills will enable you to make sure you have understood what the other person has said and demonstrate that you have heard and understood, to the other person.

| Behaviour | Definition | Example |
|---|---|---|
| **Testing understanding** | This demonstrates you have heard and understood what the other person has said. It allows the other person to correct you if there is anything you have misunderstood. For clients it is very reassuring to know you have understood correctly so it is a very positive behaviour to use in client meetings. | *"Can I check that what you are saying is that x is a priority, but y is not?"*<br>*"So in other words you are not planning to go ahead with that?"*<br>*What I think I heard was that it'll be next year now?"* |
| **Summarising** | This is where all the important facts, ideas and actions are pulled together and played back to the client. It's a very effective behaviour for getting clarity into the conversation and avoids confusion later on. | *"Let me summarise if I may. We've agreed you want to organise an employee engagement survey, report the findings back to the board and agree priorities. We also said we'd have a top team event"* |
| **Reflecting** | This focuses more on feelings you have "heard" and is a very effective behaviour for strengthening rapport and gathering an even greater depth of information. | *"I get the sense you are very frustrated with the current course of action".*<br>*"You sound very enthusiastic about that – is that right?"* |
| **Encouraging** | This behaviour essentially helps the other person to keep talking and providing the information that you need. The language is very neutral.<br>Verbal encouragement is often accompanied by non-verbal listening such as nodding and smiling. | *"That's interesting....."*<br>*"Mmmm.........*<br>*"Uh huh, tell me more..."* |

*"Selling is really about having conversations with people and helping improve their company or their life. If you look at it like that, selling is a very admirable thing to do." – Lori Richardson*

**Summary of what you have learnt in this chapter**

- **High performing sellers ask questions** – they ask more questions rather than giving information and facts.
- **They have an effective questioning framework** – questions to reinforce and build rapport, questions to explore problems and develop needs, questions to uncover needs and priorities, questions to identify decision-makers, questions to uncover decision criteria and questions to understand competitors.
- **They balance inquiry with advocacy** – as well as asking questions they use information to educate and provide unique and valuable insight for clients.
- **They use verbal listening**

# Chapter 7

## The best sales conversations balance advocacy with inquiry

There is no doubt that high performing sellers are extremely curious and have a very strong questioning style. However, it is important that your clients don't feel as though they are undergoing an inquisition. The most productive sales conversations balance inquiry (asking questions) with advocacy (providing insight and education, giving advice, telling stories). A well-planned and skilful questioning strategy combined with thought leadership, insight, education and advice for your client will help you create and deliver value to your clients and prospects.

Sales conversations require give and take. You have to get your client or prospect talking so you can fully understand their situation. You also need to take what your client or prospect says and make suggestions, offer opinions and insight, based on your expertise to help them see how you can help. In each and every sales conversation (yes, this includes capabilities presentations) you have to balance how much you talk and how much you listen.

In 2015, I worked in collaboration with Professor Chris Mckenna, who was, the director of the Centre for Professional Services at Said Business School. We looked at the models for sales and client development in law firms. During the study and in my conversations with buyers of legal services, I asked 2 questions, *"What is it that lawyers do that you really value?"* and *"What is it that you would like lawyers to do more of?"* Not surprisingly the answer was very similar and pretty much the same from all the buyers I spoke to and that was *"come to us with ideas and insight, share your experiences with us and tell us what we should be thinking about that we are not".*

This study focused on how lawyers engage with their clients, however it is my belief that this is one of the most effective ways you can create value for clients across the professional services sector.

You'll know when you have provided an alternative perspective or given them an idea they had not thought of when you hear responses such as *"That's an interesting idea, I'd not thought of that" "Mmm that's and interesting question".*

The best indicator of the value you create for clients, through your insight and education, is when they come to you to ask your opinion on something they have read or been told. While there is more information than ever available, it's the opinion and advice sought by clients that deliver the greatest value.

## Sources of insight and thought leadership

*"You may not be your clients' main source of information, but you need to be their most valuable source of information"*

There are many sources of insight available to professional firms which you can use to create value for a client or prospect.

**Horizon scanning –** Most professional service firms have programmes which track changes, such as market trends, economic and political trends, legislative and regulatory changes.

**Proprietary research –** Many firms will carry out or sponsor primary research projects. For example, one firm I worked with undertook a piece of research on the emerging risks for large businesses and institutions and these are tremendous sources of insight and potential sales opportunities. Using the findings from this type of proprietary research is a highly effective way to open doors and get to meet people you wouldn't otherwise be able to.

**Client research –** Studies undertaken by clients can be a hugely valuable source of insight and this includes customer feedback studies. Gaining access to your clients' research studies can provide a valuable source of insight for them. Insights from client feedback is very useful for gaining the commitment and buy-in to sales and client development initiative from colleagues in the firm.

**Market intelligence –** This is more widely available research such as general market research reports.

However, while the information from these different sources will be of interest, the real value for clients and prospects lies in how you use the information to help clients – to interpret and offer your opinion on what it means for them, to disrupt clients' current thinking, to offer a new perspective or to give clients the benefit of your experience.

I often see extremely detailed information, for example, about forthcoming legislative or regulatory change, which is sent out to clients or posted on LinkedIn and other social media platforms and which forms an important part of a firm's marketing communications. While this information is useful, where this information helps to create sales opportunities is when it is used to create valuable insight for clients and prospects. The more you know about your clients' and prospects' business; their strategic goals, priorities etc., the more effective you can be in using information to educate your clients and create unique and valuable insight for them.

Simply providing your clients and prospects with information and thought leadership is no longer a differentiator. Helping your clients make sense of the information you provide is what will set you apart. In Gartner's Buyers Survey they show that if a client has too much information and information that may appear contradictory, they are less likely to make decisions. Today's sellers are providing so much information that clients are often overloaded and reach saturation point such that they are unable to make informed decisions. Where sellers help clients make sense of information as they move through their buying journey, they are more likely to influence the decision in their favour. Helping clients make sense of information builds their confidence and reduces scepticism.

Professional advisers may no longer be a client's most common source of information but you must be a client's most valuable source of information and you can do this by helping them to make sense of all the information that they have.

Three distinct categories of seller behaviour were identified in Gartner's Buyers Survey 2019, in relation to how individuals share information with buyers

**Giving** – the underlying mind set here is that more is better. It is often quite a passive approach to providing information, largely in response to clients' requests.

**Telling** – this is where individuals are relying on their personal experience and knowledge in the information they provide

**Sense Making** – this is where the seller helps the clients to evaluate different sources of information reconcile contradictory information. They help the client prioritise and understand relevant information

So, what do you need to do to help clients make sense of all the information available to them?

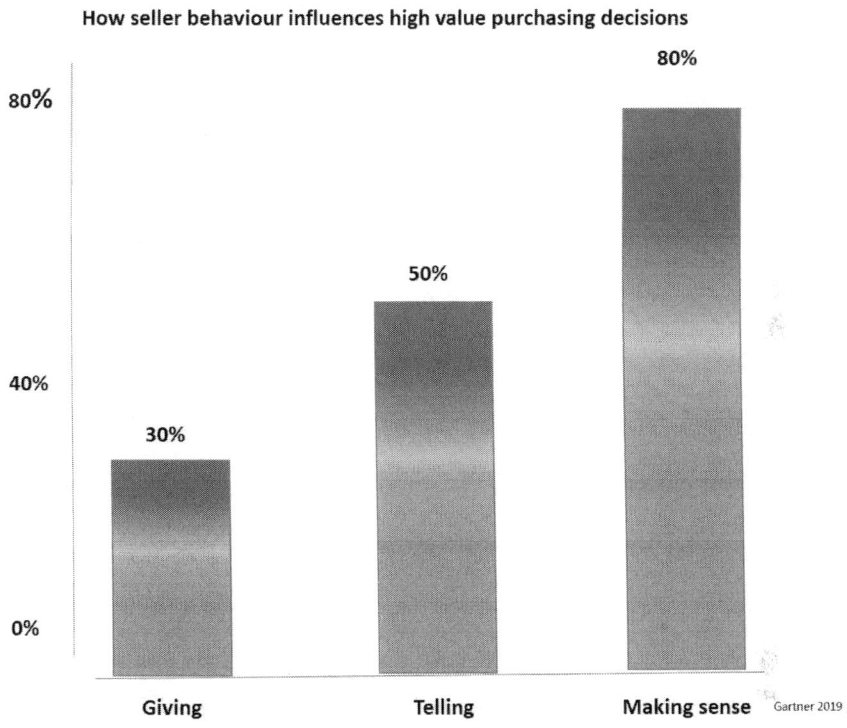


fig 14. How seller behaviour influences decision

Make sure you have a good understanding of your clients' needs and priorities, provide clients with appropriate information and make sure the client is confident that they have all the relevant information they need.

Clarify the information for the client. Reduce the complexity of the information by processing and interpreting it for them.

Finally, collaborate with your client to help them use the information to make informed decisions.

**Selling by story telling**

*"You need to be able to paint a picture in a conversation. The lost part of sales is the storytelling side." – Richard Harris*

One of the most powerful tools in your sales toolbox is the ability to tell a good story and it will materially increase your ability to influence and persuade buyers to change. This is because your stories generally draw on your personal knowledge and experience which makes them all the more convincing.

One of the biggest challenges for sellers of professional services, as I highlighted in a previous chapter, is disrupting a client or prospect's status quo bias, to persuade them to address problems they are happy to live with. Clients are significantly more risk adverse than previously and more willing to stay put – despite what may be quite high levels of dissatisfaction – simply because it's less risky. While questions help your client or prospect explore their problems and encourage them to consider the value of change, a good story will make you even more persuasive.

*"You know it's really interesting, I was with another high street retailer who had a large portfolio, all of which were leasehold. We discovered all sorts of unnecessary costs in their leases which were having a significant impact on their operating costs. We did a complete review of all their leases and renegotiated terms, where we could. As a result, we made significant reductions in both their costs and their risk."*

What this story does is bring the client's current situation to life. It illustrates how the seller helped a client explore a similar problem, found a solution and described how the client benefitted. Not only does this help the client explore their problems and needs but it also builds credibility and the reassurance that you've done it before and know what to do to help them.

**Summary of what you have learnt in this chapter**

- One of the most effective ways you can deliver value to your clients is to provide thought leadership, insight and perspectives that help the client to see a different view
- There are a number of sources of thought leadership and insight you can use to help clients
- The most effective sellers help clients make sense of the information . you may not be a client's main source of information but you need to be their most valuable source of information
- High performing sellers use stories to help clients to understand new ideas and to build credibility through social proof

# Chapter 8

## Making meetings more productive

Sales meeting with key stakeholders are often hard won – your clients are busy and often difficult to get access to. With this is mind, meetings need a purpose. Sales meetings may take a number of weeks or months to arrange, be postponed and rearranged along the way, so it's important that you make your meetings as productive as possible and useful for the client. How often have you met with a client or prospect, yet despite going with a plan and knowing what you want to talk about, somehow the client grabbed the agenda and you weren't able to achieve your objective? Did you leave the meeting feeling frustrated and wondering how you might get another meeting to talk about what you wanted to talk about?

This is a common scenario and very frustrating. While simply meeting with clients and prospects for coffee and a chat is always helpful for getting to know each other and building the relationship, you can only have, and indeed the client will only want, so many of these meetings. If your meetings lack purpose, are unproductive and of little value to the client – other than to have a chat – clients will not make time to see you. If on the other hand your meetings are productive and of value to the client, they will make time and want to see you again.

In this chapter I want to look at how you can take control of a sales meeting and lead the conversation, so that your meetings will be more productive for you, and be more interesting and of value to the client. When I say take control, I mean encouraging the client to talk about what you need them to talk about, so that you can identify and develop new business opportunities or further explore those opportunities you know exist.

*"Productive meetings are never an accident. They are the result of commitment to excellence, intelligent planning and focused efforts" – Paul J Meyer*

One of the distinguishing characteristics of high performing sellers is the ability, confidence and willingness to take control. If you go into meetings believing that the client should take the lead and do all the talking and your job is just to listen, there is a risk you will fail to meet your objective and may waste an opportunity. Of course your client must do the talking, as I said in the previous paragraph and of course you must listen, but you need to drive the meeting and lead the conversation to get the client talking about the things you need them to talk about.

**Structuring a client meeting**

Set out below is a simple framework to help you structure and lead a sales meeting to ensure you focus on the client or prospect, meet your objective and make the meeting productive.

| | Relation to success | Frequency of use | Effect |
|---|---|---|---|
| Feature | Low | Very High 37.5% | *Price concerns* |
| Advantage | Moderate | High 17.5% | *Objections* |
| Benefit | High | Low 5% | *Support* |

fig16. FAB

There are four distinct phases in a sales meeting. Each phase has a specific purpose, to help you to achieve your objectives.

**Phase 1 – Opening the meeting – getting started and positioning yourself to lead the conversation**

The opening phase, which should only be a few minutes, allows you to set out the road map for the meeting and manage client expectations. There are five things you need to focus on in the opening phase of the meeting.

- Preliminaries
- People
- Process
- Purpose
- Permissions

Let's look at each of these in a bit more detail.

***Preliminaries***

This is the "chit-chat" part of the meeting and is particularly important if there are people in the meeting you don't know. People do business with people they like, so spending time building rapport is an important part of the meeting. A word of warning here: be observant and aware of the expectations of the people you meet, when it comes to chit-chat. Some people enjoy chit-chat while others prefer to get down to business and it's important to adopt the appropriate social style at the outset of a meeting, to build rapport.

If people are meeting you for the first time, it's important to establish some initial credibility early in the meeting. With this in mind it's useful to provide a short value proposition (you may have heard this described as your **elevator pitch**). The emphasis is on brevity. If you prepare this before the meeting, you will avoid launching into a long-winded and uninteresting sales pitch. Furthermore, preparing your value proposition ahead of the meeting will enable you to tailor it to the audience. Your value proposition should focus on how you help, not what you do. People don't want to know that you have 80 partners, have been in business since 1820 or that you have prestigious offices in the city centre. What they do want to know is what you can do for them – for example:

> *"I don't know how much you know about our firm but as a retailer, you may be interested to know that retail is one of our biggest sectors and we run a number of research projects looking at various trends in the market - such as consumer buying trends."*

> *""Most of the time we work with small businesses to help them achieve their growth plans"*

> *"Our firm specialises in helping companies to improve the productivity of their teams"*

Finally there is the "bear pit" to be aware of and deal with appropriately. This is when the client jumps in at the outset of the meeting and asks questions such as *"So how can you help us?" or "What do you think you can do, that our current suppliers aren't doing?", "What do you think we should be doing?"*

What can happen at this point is that you are lured into making an early and most likely generic sales pitch, which may not be of interest to the client. The response here is to regain control of the meeting.

> *"There are a number of ways I think we can help you, but I'd like to ask you a few questions first so that what I talk to you about will be relevant"*

***People***

You may well go to meetings at which you will meet people from the client organisation, who you've not met before, or you may go to a meeting and take a colleague that the client doesn't know. You need to know who people are, but more importantly, why they are attending the meeting.

I went to a meeting recently and met someone from the L&D team that I was not expecting to meet. I asked her if there was anything she'd particularly like from the meeting and discovered she was the business partner for one of the client's subsidiaries. They were looking at training the sales force, which is why she had come along. She was introduced by the head of L&D as "this is my colleague, Tricia". I'm glad I asked, it changed the agenda of the meeting!

***Purpose***

This part of the opening is about managing your client or prospect's expectations in terms of what you want talk to them about. It's important that you also ask them what they want to talk about. I suggest sending out an agenda before the meeting. It doesn't need to be a highly formal agenda, a simple email should be fine:

*"I'm looking forward to our meeting next week and I'm just planning ahead. I'd like to follow up on our discussion at last week's seminar and the issues you said you were having, following the recent acquisition. Is there anything in particular you'd like to discuss?"*

Setting up an agenda ahead of the meeting demonstrates to the client that you are prepared. Furthermore, if they do come back to you with the things they want to discuss, you can do some preparation ahead of the meeting.

***Process***

At some point you need to confirm how much time you have and agree with your client or prospect how you'd like to use the time.

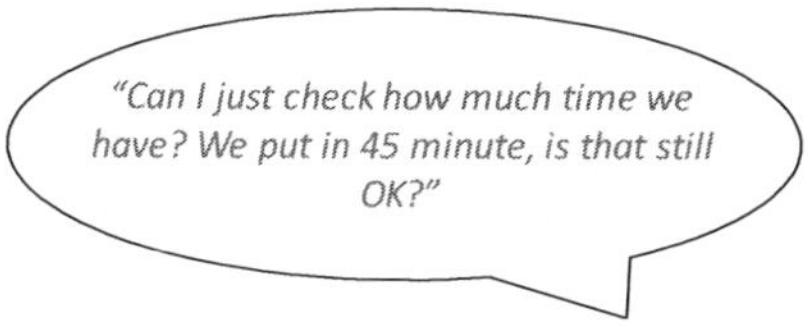


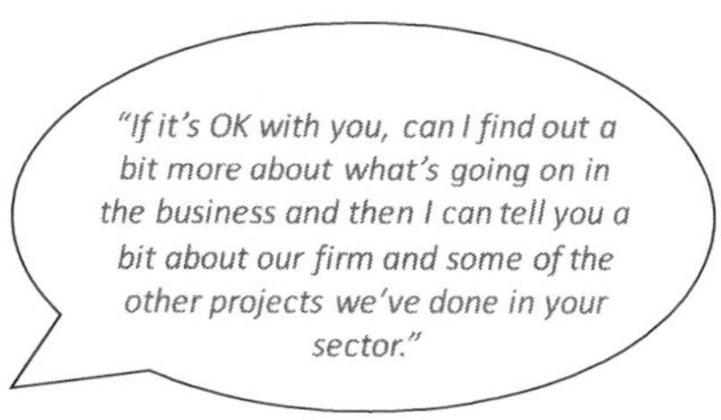

If you don't check timings there is always a risk the client or prospect will suddenly announce another meeting they have to leave for, which has come up since you set up the meeting. If that happens and the meeting comes to a rapid close, you have lost control of the process and getting a good outcome from the meeting will be difficult!

***Permission***

Believe it or not, people worry about taking notes. In a routine service delivery meeting, it's second nature to take notes. Yet somehow, in a sales meeting, there are all sorts of concerns.

*"Will the client think I'm not listening?", "How can I take notes and listen to the clients?"*

As you open the meeting, just say to the client that you'll take some notes, so that you don't miss anything important. Just make sure you have a notebook and pen to hand to avoid rummaging around in your bag once the meeting has begun. Some people take notes on a laptop or iPad – personally, I feel that does reduce your engagement with the client and ability to lead the conversation, but that is a personal viewpoint.

I will be coming back to note-taking later in the chapter and suggesting an easy way to take notes while continuing to lead the conversation.

**Phase 2 - Investigating – uncovering, clarifying and developing client needs and gathering other information critical for sales success**

This is the most important phase of a sales meeting. As the name suggests, it is the part of the meeting where you are focused on asking questions and uncovering the critical information you need, to identify and progress new business opportunities.

Individuals who are successful in winning business are CURIOUS and the longer you remain curious the more information you will gather about your client's business.

Set out below is the information that you need to gather during a sales meeting in order to progress any new business opportunity, which we call your "Fuel". Use this as a guide to develop your questions in meetings. Remember you may not get all of the information you need in one meeting, so keeping track of the information you have and the information you need, is a critical element in developing new business opportunities.

- ***Emerging needs*** – These are the problems, concerns and frustrations that a client expresses and may become their future needs, so you should uncover and explore them with the client. But remember clients live with problems, so these problems may not yet be a priority for clients.
  e.g. *"I am worried about the increasing amounts of regulation", "the constant changes in legislation cause us a real headache."*
- ***Explicit needs*** – These are your client's immediate priorities in terms of what they want to do and you should focus on these first.
  e.g. *"I need to look at our employment contracts", "I want to make certain we review the contracts first."*
- ***Decision-makers and decision-making process*** – Decision-making is increasingly complex and you need to know the role your client contact has in making or influencing the decision in order to adopt the right strategy.
- ***Decision Criteria*** – In most decisions a client is about to make, they will be considering your competitors as well as you. Clients use Decision Criteria (DC) to evaluate and compare competing suppliers.
- ***Competitors*** – Who are they and how does your client view them? It is important to understand how your client sees the relative strengths and weaknesses of you and your competitors.

A word of warning, during the investigating phase of a meeting, your client may well reveal some really valuable information. Try not to be tempted away from investigating too quickly, or you could miss important opportunities. However, it is important to acknowledge something your client or prospect may want to discuss with you and that you intend to return to.

You also need to be aware of what to do if the client starts to ask you too many questions. It is easy to believe that when the client starts to ask questions, it is a good sign. When this happens, the risk is you keep answering the client or prospect's questions and providing them with information they need and then not getting what you need. However, you need to know why the client is seeking information, so it's important to regain control.

This way you can find out about their underlying needs or problems and ensure that what you say is more relevant and interesting.

**Phase 3 – Presenting solutions – Showing how you can help**

This is the part of the meeting where you will be presenting ideas and solutions to clients and your principal focus is to ensure whatever you present to clients or prospects addresses the needs you have explored with them.

There are three ways in which you can describe your capability to clients;

- Features
- Advantages
- Benefits

**Features** – Describe the characteristics of the organisation and your services:

*"We have 120 partners"*

*"We have offices in eight European centres"*

Features generally offer no value to clients and so in the client's mind your solution will seem expensive and result in price concerns.

Features are easy to use and people generally feel comfortable, consequently frequent use of features when selling to clients is high – yet their persuasive power is very low and if used too much will actually irritate the client.

**Advantages** – These are a slightly more persuasive way to describe your capability to clients as there is an attempt to place some value for the client or establish a competitive advantage.

Advantages may be appealing to a client as they can help to shape their needs. They may also help to build credibility with a client early in their decision-making

Later on, when a client's needs are more established, advantages are less appealing and are likely to result in objections.

**Benefit statements** – The most persuasive way to describe your capability because they address specific needs.

*"From what you said earlier, cost transparency is critical and we can provide this by using our technology platform for managing lease renewals".*

The most important factor when presenting solutions to clients is that they are tailored to meet your client's needs. We often think we are tailoring our solutions when in fact we are not, either because we are making assumptions about our clients' needs or we don't hear them and therefore it may not be clear to clients how our solutions will address their needs.

The key to tailoring solutions is to be sure you fully understand your clients' needs and make it explicitly clear how your solution meets their needs and the benefits they are looking for.

- Uncover and develop clients' problems
- Get the clients to express **Needs**
- Build value for a solution

Then you can offer the client benefits which demonstrate how your solution can satisfy their needs.

***Social Proof***

Use of "social proof" is helpful in gaining the commitment of your clients and prospects – clients want to know how you can help and how they will be better off and I'll look at this again in more detail when we look at how to enhance the persuasive value of a presentation.

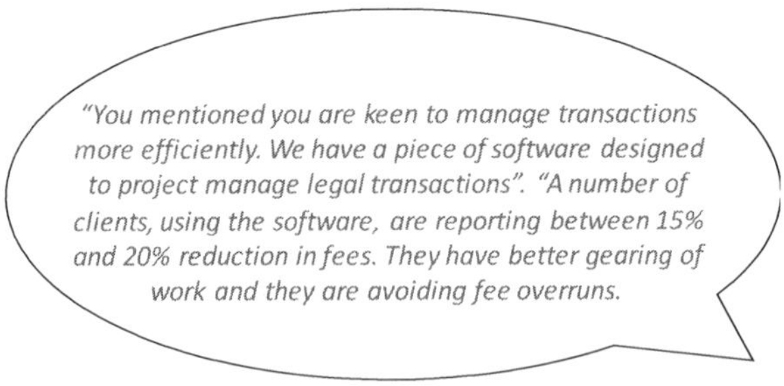


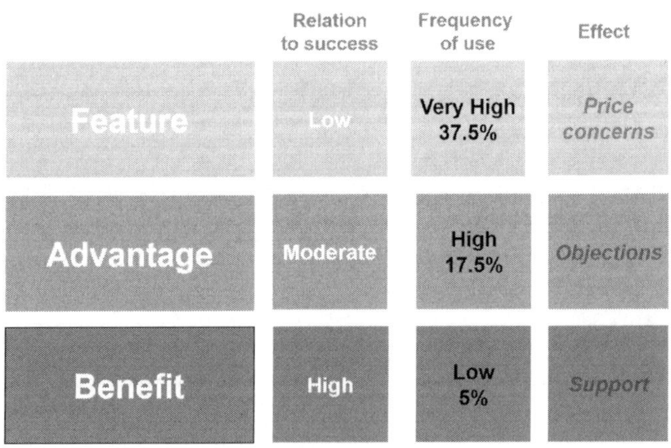


fig16. FAB

### Phase 4 – Closing the meeting – obtaining commitment

Selling professional services is known as a complex or major sale. This means clients and prospects may take weeks, months or even longer to make decisions. It is very rare that you will go to a meeting and walk away with an instruction – indeed some studies suggest that less than 1 in 10 sales meetings close with an instruction. Equally, it is highly unlikely you will get an outright rejection. So it is important that you obtain an appropriate outcome at the end of a sales meeting that will enable you to progress the new business opportunities that you have identified.

#### *Meeting outcomes*

A **continuation** is an outcome where there is no commitment or agreement from the client or prospect to any action that moves towards a sale. Invariably it is the seller that commits their time and resource to any action. However, the relationship continues. Typical continuations include:

- Seller commits to send a proposal or fee quote
- The seller commits to provide more information
- The seller commits to invite the buyer and other colleagues to a seminar

One of the traps individuals fall into at the end of a meeting is to be over optimistic about continuations. When a client asks you for a fee proposal or more information, it is not a buying signal. It's more likely that the client is being polite, so be ready to turn advances into continuations in order to help progress opportunities.

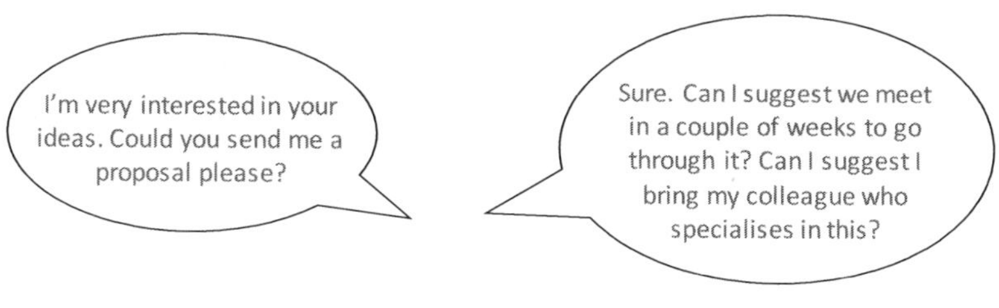


An **advance** is an outcome where the client or prospect commits to an action that moves you closer to a sale. Typical advances include:

- The client or prospect agreeing to another meeting
- They agree to meet your colleague
- They agree to introduce you to other people in their organisation
- They agree to send you a request for a proposal

The more advances you get over a period of time, the more likely it is that you will achieve a successful sales outcome.

**Planning Advances**

High performing sellers consistently plan and manage their sales meetings so that they can move sales opportunities forward in realistic stages. For each meeting they consider a variety of advances that would move them forward towards a sale, and then plan around the actions they believe the client or prospect are most likely to agree to.

The following example shows how you might plan for advances, ahead of the meeting.

**A case in point...**

The firm is currently trying to get onto the panel for a new client, to provide a range of outsourced services, including payroll, IT and facilities management. The prospect is a large manufacturing business with five divisions, all UK based. The firm's key contact is one member in a six-member selection board which includes the divisional heads and the company's chief operating officer. The tender will take place sometime in the next 12 months. This is the first sales meeting with the project leader.

***Possible Advances***

- A follow up meeting with other divisional directors;
- A meeting between the head of outsourcing and the COO – possibly via a thought leadership breakfast on trends in outsourcing;
- Introductions of others in our team to project lead;
- Get the project lead to contact two other outsourcing clients;
- Training/thought leadership event for member of the selection board;
- Get the project leaders to come to a forthcoming seminar on outsourcing.

Many less successful sellers are happy with outcomes such as *"We collected some really interesting information", "Everyone in the meeting got on really well", "They really liked our approach and felt it would be really helpful in the future", "They are interested in our training."*

There is nothing wrong with these outcomes; relationships are key to successful selling in the professional services sector but there is no action that will move the sale forward.

High performing sellers plan for and achieve more advances. To do this they spend time and manage the investigating phase of the meeting effectively. Furthermore, they plan for meetings and focus on the key information they need to identify and progress new business opportunities.

Set out below is a simple meeting plan to help you focus on the investigating phase of your meeting and increase your chance of getting a good advance. You should have an idea of the questions you want to ask and that enable you to lead the conversation, but you also need to remain flexible and be able to respond to what your client tells you.

**Objective (Advance):** explore current challenges and get a follow up meeting to meet other stakeholders and introduce at least one other colleague

| Key information you need to identify and progress opportunities | Questions you need to ask to uncover and clarify information |
|---|---|
| **Needs** | Plan a series of questions to uncover and clarify current needs and priorities. Explore what might stop them achieving their priorities (see chapter 5). |
| **Emerging needs** | Plan a series of questions to uncover and develop their emerging needs. What problems are they living with, how significant are those problems and what is the impact if they don't do anything is a framework of questions that will help you to do this. (See chapter 5) |
| **Decision Criteria** | You need to find out about the criteria they will use to select and compare suppliers. |
| **Decision-makers** | You need to know who will make, influence and scrutinise decisions. |
| **Competitors** | Find out about competitors and their relative strengths and weaknesses. |
| **Key business information** | Ask about any changes that may be on the horizon – internally or externally and what the impact may be.<br><br>Gather key business information you need that you can't get from other sources. |

Source:

**Meeting notes**

Taking an accurate set of notes will ensure you can progress any new business opportunities. Good notes will also help you to brief colleagues. This may be necessary if you are passing information back to others who work with the client, or if you are briefing a colleague for a meeting they will be attending with the client.

It's not necessary to prepare a verbatim set of notes, but it is important that you capture the information needed to progress any opportunities you identify with a client.

A good way to ensure you record the information you need to and stay in control of the meeting is to pre-catalogue your information. This way you can abbreviate the notes you take, but they will still make sense afterwards.

You will know if the meeting has gone as you planned, if your meeting plan and your meeting notes are aligned. It's a simple and effective test of how well you have taken control and led the meeting.

Set out below is a suggested method **for effective note-taking**

| Emerging needs<br>(Frustrations, dissatisfactions and things that worry the client. Not necessarily looking for solutions. Clients live with problems, so these are emerging needs) |
|---|
| Needs<br>(These are the client's priorities and they are probably exploring solutions) |
| Decision criteria<br>(The basis they will use for selecting suppliers e.g. sector knowledge, price, leverage of work) |
| Decision-makers and decision-making process<br>(These are the people who will make and/or influence decisions and how the decision will be made e.g. formal tender) |
| Competitors<br>(Who they are and their relative strengths and weaknesses) |
| Key information<br>(Changes in the business, key financial information, strategic goals etc.) |

### Use your routine meetings with clients to win business

In this chapter we've been talking about how to structure a sales meeting. Dedicated sales meetings with clients and prospects are a vital and often under-used business development activity. However, one of the other really useful sales opportunities is routine service delivery meetings with clients, which means you don't need to find additional time to speak to clients and prospects over and above your fee earning time. We call this "sales through service". It is one of your best BD opportunities and is a well-recognised and well-utilised sales opportunity in other sectors – particularly business services where, similar to professional services, sales and service delivery are integrated.

Most clients will be happy to allow you to explore other opportunities with them or provide you with any information you need to help you develop the relationship with them. It's important to set it up before the meeting and make sure any time you spend on business development is "off the clock".

*"There are a couple of other things I'd like to explore with you in our meeting next week, if that's OK?"*

*"We are seeing some interesting trends in your sector I'd like to share with you in our meeting".*

**Summary of what you have learnt in this chapter**

- Take control of the sales process and lead the conversation.
- Manage the **four phases** of the sales meeting effectively.
- Your focus in the **Investigating Phase** should be to uncover and explore your client's needs and gather the other information you need to progress new business opportunities.
- Don't rush on too quickly into the next phase which is **Presenting Solutions** or you may end up with a "feature dump".
- **Benefit Statements** are the most persuasive way of demonstrating capability as they address the client's' **Explicit Needs** and give them what they want.
- Use **Social Proof** to reinforce the value of your solutions.
- Plan for **Advances** so that you can maintain momentum and progress opportunities.
- Take accurate notes so that you can progress opportunities but also brief colleagues accurately.

# Chapter 9

## Are you talking to the right people?

Having worked in an operational sales and client management role for the last 5 years, and prior to that as a consultant with many of the top law firms, I recently found myself asking: why is selling into complex organisations so much more difficult now? Why do decisions take so much longer? and why is it that opportunities that look incredibly positive seem to end in "no decision"? Or, worse still, despite being led to believe you are the chosen supplier, a competitor comes from left field and for some reason gets the decision to go their way?

One of the principle factors, which makes selling professional services complicated (and frustrating), is the number and diversity of people involved in making or influencing the decision.

The graph below from research undertaken by the Corporate Executive Board (CEB) clearly illustrates how the likelihood of a decision being made declines rapidly as the number of decision-makers increases. What this study also found was that the majority of business to business decisions (B2B) now involve an average of 5.4 people and at least one of those people may be from the C-suite – a board level executive. Board level executives (BLE) generally leave decision-making on operational matters – such as which professional adviser to appoint for a transaction or who to appoint to a panel, to others in the business. However, if they see decisions being made that they don't like, they will intervene and say "No".

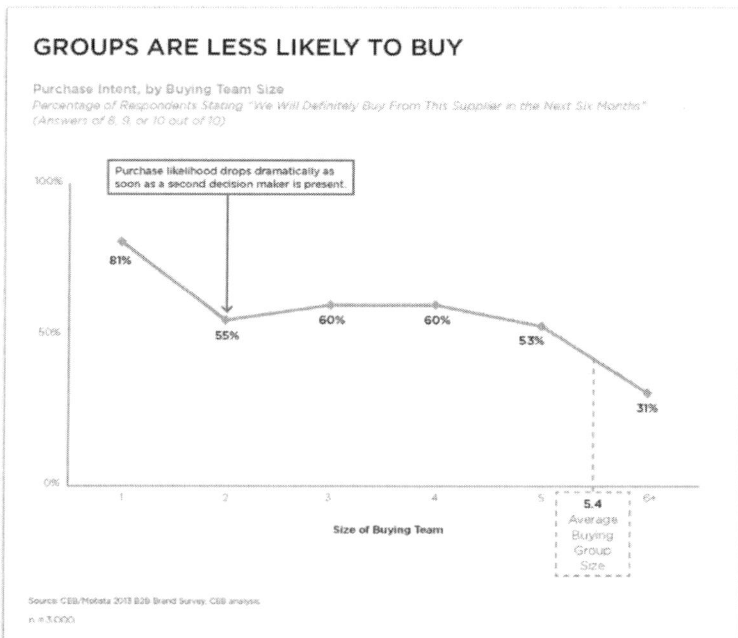


fig 17. Groups less likely to buy

In this chapter I am going to describe the different types of buyer you need to recognise and engage with. I will also explore strategies for navigating the stakeholder network in the client organisation, to enhance your influence and competitor advantage.

Your success depends on making sure you know who makes, influences and scrutinises decisions in the client organisations you are working with.

### The sellers' landscape has changed

Let's start by looking at some of the changes in the seller's landscape and the changes in clients' buying behaviour, which has driven the need for sellers to behave differently in order to win business and attract new clients.

**Today's buyers of professional services:**

- Have access to information – primarily through the internet – that only a few years ago they would have relied on their advisers to provide, so gaining access is more difficult;
- Are in a much more complex network of stakeholders who have an influence over decisions;
- Are more inclined to engage with suppliers later in their decision-making, making it more difficult for advisers to influence buyers;
- Are more sophisticated and only want to spend time and talk to advisers who can provide them with value, in the form of insights and other information they don't know;
- Are increasingly sceptical and risk adverse;
- Have to be more collaborative and they need to be able to gain the commitment and support of others to make decisions and get budget approved.

The increased sophistication of buyers and the complexity of decision-making means that sellers of professional services need to have a much greater understanding of who makes and influences decisions. They also need to be able to navigate the stakeholder network effectively, to build relationships and influence the right people.

When exploring with individuals or teams the reasons for losing out on a sales opportunity, the response tends to be *"the other firm had better sector knowledge"*, *"they were cheaper than us"* or *"we've decided that now is not the right time"*. These are undoubtedly genuine reasons. However, in today's environment, simply not having the right connections may mean the decision may not go your way or you lose out to competitors who are better connected.

The challenge you have is that the people who are accessible and with whom you have day-to-day contact, may not be the people who can make the decision. However, you don't have access to others who will have greater influence over the final decision.

The first thing to recognise is that complex purchasing decisions are no longer made by just one or two people. These decisions are made by "Buying Groups" – groups which consist of a number of people who can make or influence buying decisions.

The Corporate Executive Board (CEB), now Gartner, ran a study where they analysed 700 stakeholders across hundreds of client organisations – all involved in the purchase of high value goods and services. The purpose of the study was to see how effective each type of stakeholder was in influencing decisions and also gaining consensus with others. A major factor for sellers of professional services, which will determine how successful you are, is the ability to understand and influence the buying group that will be making decisions.

What I often see is individuals or client teams gathering organisational charts and information about stakeholders' functional responsibilities. However, they don't necessarily have an accurate picture of individuals' influence and political power in their organisation.

An example I use is a firm of management consultants I worked with, who were selling a new performance management system. They worked closely with members of the prospect's HR team, including the head of HR, scoping out what was required and designing the solution. They made presentations to various parts of the business and the budget as agreed. After 6 months there was still no progress, despite my client being promised they were the preferred supplier. So, we took another look at the organisational chart, to see if there were gaps in their connections. They also asked their principle contacts what was stopping this project going ahead. It seemed they were having difficulty getting the commitment from other parts of the business, some of whom were questioning whether a new performance management system was a priority. The HR team reported into the Chief Operations director and my client ended up working with the HR team to present the proposed solution with clear evidence of the business benefits to the COO. Four months later my client got the green light. The assumption that was made for six months was that the head of HR had sufficient political influence to gain the necessary consensus to get the project over the line, which proved to be a flawed assumption.

## Questions that buyers need to ask

A key focus for your questioning strategy needs to find out about how decisions are made and by whom. Listed below are some examples of questions which will help you to do this.

- Do we know who will be making the decision?
- Can we recognise their different roles?
- Is there a champion for this project?
- Is there anyone who might say "no"?
- Can we get/do we have access to this person?
- What are the drivers/what's important for the different stakeholders who will make this decision?
- Who are our competitors speaking to?
- Who and what may stop us winning this business?
- Who else can help us to gain influence with the buying group?

One of the most important questions you need to ask, as I have highlighted in this list is *"Who could say no" "what might lead them to say no?"*

**A case in point ...**

I was working with a large insurance and shipping law firm helping them to win a pitch for a very high-profile real estate client. They undoubtedly had the capability to do the work, however, I was a bit worried that as a well-known insurance and shipping brand there might be someone who felt they weren't the right firm. I asked the question – Is there anyone who might say no? The team I was working with felt that they knew who all the decision-makers were and felt comfortable that all was well. They did a fantastic pitch and were appointed as the preferred supplier. However, at the last minute, the CEO joined the discussion and said he wasn't happy that the firm was an insurance and shipping firm and asked that a mainstream commercial firm be appointed.

C-suite executives generally scrutinise decisions from a risk perspective and if they feel a decision may be risky, for whatever reason that will be, they say "no".

### 7 types of buyers

The CEB identified that stakeholders fall into one of seven buyer types. Individual buyers can fall into one or more of each type, in other words they are not mutually exclusive. Then, you need the right strategy for influencing each of these buyers.

Outlined below is a description of each of these different stakeholder types which, no doubt, you'll recognise from your experience in working with your own clients.

#### The Go-Getter

These people are focused on business improvement and are interested in any ideas that will help them achieve that. They will quickly become the champions of good people with good ideas when they find them— no matter where they come from. What's more, **Go-Getters** deliver results.

#### The Sceptic

These people are also interested in business improvement, but they are more sceptical about new ideas and often need more convincing that a new idea – however compelling – can be implemented successfully. Even if they are championing a new idea, sceptics are more challenging and will readily push back and demand significant amounts of evidence to be convinced. Often, they'll start with the assumption *"this won't work".* A conversation with a sceptic can be very uncomfortable and leave you believing they are unconvinced about you or your idea. Often what they are challenging is *"can we make this work in our organisation?"*

#### The Teacher

The Teacher's priority is to share insights and ideas and they too are interested in suggestions that will lead to business improvements. Colleagues seek them out for their advice and input. They are often the visionaries in a client organisation. Not surprisingly, they are powerful champions to have on board as they are great communicators and are good at convincing others to do things.

These first three stakeholder types are often collectively referred to as "**Mobilisers"** because they get things done. Selling successfully to mobilisers requires a very client-centric conversation focused on insights and new ideas for improving their business. They are not interested in being sold products and services, they are interested in business improvement – first and foremost. Mobilisers get decisions made by working with colleagues to get consensus. They manage the politics and share their vision internally. Conversations can be very uncomfortable because

Mobilisers will push back, demand evidence, challenge claims. To the average seller this does not feel like someone on their side but high performing sellers love engaging with Mobilisers. Mobilisers put the business first rather than the relationship they have with the supplier – although they recognise that others in the business need to have a good relationship with them. They are the champions of new ideas and make things happen. If there is no champion for the opportunity you are pursuing or you can't gain access to a mobiliser, the likelihood of success is slim. Look at the decisions that have been made quickly and in your favour – the chances are there was a strong and influential champion.

The problem for sellers is that they are rarely visible or accessible during the decision-making process.

**The Friend**

The Friend is readily accessible to sellers and are generally interesting people to spend time with. They are happy to introduce sellers to other stakeholders in the organisation. The Friend is happy to make time to meet with people from outside their organisation and is often very supportive and apparently committed to the seller's ideas and proposals. It is very easy to be overly optimistic about the influence and ability of such people to make decisions.

**The Guide**

The Guide has very little influence or ability to make decisions. However, they are extremely useful when pursuing a new business opportunity. These people are helpful because they have and are invariably willing to share useful information. Often, this will be confidential and privileged information. Because they are seen as people "in the know." Often, the perception is that they are more senior and important than they actually are. So, again sellers are overly optimistic about their influence and ability to make decisions. These people may be outside the organisation. For example, if you are targeting a large corporate or institutional client, contact other advisers who work with them or contact former employees. I don't think you can ever have too many guides to help you influence decision-making. So, for any major purchasing decision you are trying to influence find at least one guide to help you.

**The Climber**

The Climber is focused almost entirely on personal gain. These are the people who actively back projects that raise their profile and increase their influence. When they back a project or initiative, they do so out of the belief that— if it goes well— they will be rewarded for their success. The Climber also likes to brag about past successes and accomplishments.

We refer to these three stakeholders as **"Talkers".** Unlike mobilisers, they CAN'T get things done, even though they would like to. However, as we have already identified, a lot of sellers are far too optimistic about how influential they are. This is because they are accessible, happy to spend time with sellers, prepared to share information, they understand many of the challenges their business faces and are able to make introductions. In the early weeks they may well appear to actively drive forward new initiatives. Consequently, sellers spend a lot of time with Talkers. However, they are often not sufficiently influential or skilled enough at gaining consensus among other more influential stakeholders (mobilisers).

The CEB study showed that **Talkers** are 4-6 times less able to build consensus for a purchase compared to **Mobilisers.**

What is more worrying is that over 30% of talkers are senior executives – with whom sellers have great conversations followed by empty commitments

**Friends, Guides, Climbers** and sadly **Blockers** (described below) are the people who have day-to-day operational involvement with suppliers and are therefore more visible and accessible.

**The Blocker**

Finally, the "Blocker", which as the name suggests is the stakeholder that will actively avoid change even if the benefits are clear. They work hard to defend the status quo because they prefer stability and continuity and actively seek to prevent new initiatives that would bring change and disruption. As a result, they rarely help suppliers and almost never go out of their way to speak to outside sellers. There are various reasons why these stakeholders actively block change. It could be because they "own" the system that you are looking to change or improve, they may feel threatened or they may simply like the easy life.

As with the talkers you may find blockers are your principle contacts in a client organisation but if you have an effective network within the client organisation you will be less dependent on them.

As I mentioned earlier, most stakeholders will have attributes from more than one of the buyer types described above, but it is unlikely that one buyer will have the attributes of them all.

So, the key to influencing high value purchasing decisions and winning business is to not only build strong relationships but build strong relationships with the right people who have the desire to change and have the ability and influence to gain consensus.

If your main contacts are Talkers, use these people to provide the information you need, to help you build your network and get access to the people you need to meet.

> I recently carried out a win/loss/no decision analysis on 25 opportunities pursued in the last 24 months.
>
> Where decisions were relatively quick and in my favour, I was in touch and had a relationship with a **Mobiliser**. Where I didn't win the work, it was because I didn't have access or enough influence with a mobiliser. Where decisions had stalled in my pipeline, I revisited the stakeholders I knew and was working with and developed a new account navigation strategy to gain more access, visibility and influence with mobilisers.

So, ask yourself three questions:

- Do you have access to and are you influencing the mobilisers?
- Are you spending too much time selling to talkers in the belief they can and will make a decision in your favour?
- Are your day-to-day contacts happy to live with the status quo and the familiarity around decision-makers**?**

**A case in point…**

One of the prospects on my target list was a large global law firm. They'd been on my list for a while, but I hadn't pursued them as I didn't know anyone there I could get access to. Then someone I knew well and who I had worked with from another client, moved into a business development role. We met for coffee and she told me she was keen to improve the sales effectiveness of the partners in the industry group she worked in. We had a couple of very positive meetings after which she asked me for a proposal. She wanted to take my proposal back to the group head, who she thought would readily buy into the project.

Meanwhile she also introduced me to her boss, who I met and who also appeared very supportive of the idea that developing partners' selling skills would be a good idea. I followed up and we stayed in touch, including meeting for coffee from time to time, but after a number of months of "No Progress", the project appeared to have lost momentum. I began to recognise that the people I was engaging with on this project were "Talkers" – friendly, accessible, enthusiastic about the proposal, willing to make introductions and set up meetings but unable to get the commitment of others to the project.

About the same time as I was considering whether or not to continue to pursue this client, a new global head of L&D was appointed. I didn't know her, so gaining access directly would be extremely difficult. I had a relationship with the global head of marketing, which was independent of the two people I was working on with on the partner support programme. We'd never done any work together, but we had met at conferences and in fact had shared a speaker slot at one event. I asked if she could introduce me to the new head of L&D, which she did.

Timing was on my side, as the new head of L&D happened to have "sales effectiveness" on her agenda and had convinced others in the business of its importance. The scope of the project was expanded, and I got the green light within 4 months.

## Stakeholder navigation – Power and alignment

Selling successfully and developing business in complex client organisations is about more than understanding their needs and having great solutions to meet them. You also need a detailed understanding of the stakeholder network and the ability to navigate around it, so that you can maximise your influence with the right people at the right time on the right issues.

To start with, you need to know all the people who can make, influence or scrutinise the buying decisions you are interested in. To establish an accurate picture of a client's stakeholder network it must include the people you don't know as well as those you don't. Be prepared to ask the people you are closest to in the client organisation to help you by giving you this information.

As well as knowing who can make, influence or scrutinise decisions, you also need to understand the relative power of stakeholders and where this power comes from and you also need to know how they're aligned towards you, the firm and your solutions.

Finally, you need to understand the political alliances – who gets on and is influenced by who and vice versa – where are there tensions between people. Understanding and tapping into these political alliances should form an important part of your account navigation strategy.

Mapping **Power and Alignment** in this way will help you to understand your client's stakeholder network and plan your account navigation strategy to gain access to key stakeholders and enhance your influence in the client organisation.

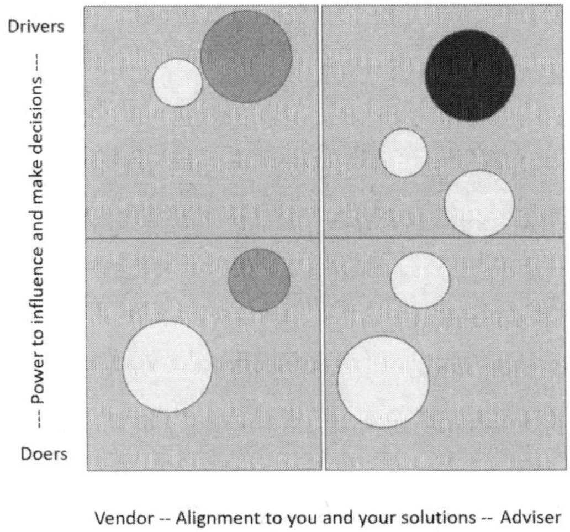


fig 18. Power & alignment

**Indicators of power**

- Have they got positional power?
- Are they someone who others consult?
- Do others think they have power?
- Are they involved in strategic projects?
- Do they have budgetary responsibility or access to discretionary funds?
- Can they achieve consensus with others and get things done?

**Indicators of alignment**

- Are they accessible?
- Are they willing to help you and your colleagues?
- Will they give you time?
- Do they support you internally with others?
- Do they come to you for advice and help?
- Are they generally supportive in their behaviour towards you?

Once you have completed the **Power and Alignment** map for a client, the next step is to identify which of your colleagues know and have relationships with which stakeholders. Generally speaking, where the firm is working with large complex organisations such as public bodies, large corporate institutions, banks, there are a number of people from different areas of the firm who either work with the client or have a relationship with them. Unfortunately, the way in which a lot of professional firms operate in silos means that it is not always clear who has relationships with a client organisation. So, as well as a detailed picture of the client's stakeholder network, you also need to know, who knows who in the firm. We call this "Man Mapping" and this information is vital for planning an effective account navigation strategy.

In chapter 15, I will explore how to win more business from existing clients and introduce a number of account development tools to help you to do this. In that chapter we will look at how to develop an effective account navigation strategy to enhance your influence with clients.

**Engaging with the C-suite**

As I touched on at the beginning of this chapter, there is one particular group of people within a client organisation which is increasingly important in influencing the decision to appoint professional advisers – be that for a transaction or advisory work – and that is the C-suite. The C-suite is the collective term for board level executives and while they may not directly make decisions, they scrutinise and evaluate the decisions that others make.

The C-suite includes:

- Chief Executive officer (CEO)
- Chief Finance officer (CFO)
- Chief Information officer (CIO)
- Chief Marketing officer (CMO)
- Chief Operations officer (COO)
- Chief Procurement officer (CPO)

One of the distinguishing characteristics of individuals who seem to be blessed with continual success at winning business and acquiring new clients, is their ability to engage effectively with the C-suite.

When thinking about how to engage with the C-suite you need to consider three questions:

- How do you know when a board level executive (BLE) would be receptive to meeting you?
- What is the most effective way to get access to a BLE?
- What do you need to talk about to ensure the meeting is successful? The opportunity cost is extremely high. If you don't deliver value to the BLE, you won't get another chance.

Let's look at when might a BLE be interested in meeting you.

The best opportunity and the one where you are most likely to be able to deliver the value BLEs look for is when the status quo starts to unravel and they may begin to be aware of new challenges and priorities. Changes in legislation or regulation, mergers and acquisitions, disposals, changing market trends all create disruption in a business, which will, in most cases, lead to some level of involvement of the board executives.

This is a real window of opportunity and a real chance for you to shape their thinking by giving them ideas they hadn't thought of and information they weren't aware of. This is where effective use of thought leadership and customer insight can deliver great value to a BLE and will help you cement your relationship with them. If a BLE believes you can help them to understand or diagnose a problem that may be hindering their progress, they will be willing to see you.

Another opportunity to engage with members of the C-suite is if you know the organisation is embarking on a major purchasing decision. For example, this may be a decision about who to appoint to a panel or preferred supplier list, or the appointment of new auditors, or it may be a decision related to a specific transaction. The earlier you can begin to get to know the board members who are involved, the better.

The third opportunity is at the point at which a major purchasing decision is about to be made – such as the agreement of which advisers will be appointed to the panel for the next few years or which firm will advise on the directors' tax affairs. At this point in the decision-making process, BLEs may be involved to scrutinise the decision to ensure they are happy and comfortable with what is being proposed. To be honest, if you leave engaging with the C-suite to this point in the decision, you are too late. Furthermore, it is highly likely that your competitors may have engaged with board members a lot earlier and are therefore, potentially, in a stronger position.

The next challenge is how to get a meeting. The most effective route into a BLE is via the introduction from a "Credible Sponsor". This is someone internally within the client organisation that the BLE knows and respects. There may also be credible sponsors outside the organisation who could help you get access to a C-suite executive.

| Tactics to gain access to board level executives | Always | Usually | Occasionally | Never |
|---|---|---|---|---|
| Introduction by a sponsor in the company | 16% | 68% | 16% | 0% |
| Introduction by someone outside the company | 8% | 36% | 44% | 12% |
| Email followed by a call | 4% | 20% | 40% | 36% |
| Cold call | 0% | 20% | 36% | 44% |
| Contact at an off site event | 0% | 44% | 32% | 24% |

Source: Gaining access to board level executives (Read and Bistritz).

So, what do you need to do to get introductions from credible sponsors? Firstly, you need to identify the "credible sponsor" and if this is someone you know then the next step is to approach them. Be careful it doesn't look as though you are going directly over their head as this may be counterproductive. Consider these approaches:

- Use your sponsor to invite them to a round table event on a piece of thought leadership where they might meet other industry leaders. This may also enhance your sponsor's profile.
- Ask a colleague if they have a "credible sponsor" who would make an introduction.
- Find a credible sponsor elsewhere in the business whom you know can introduce you.

The most effective account navigation strategies require you and your colleagues to work together to access the right people

**What to talk about with a BLE**

The first thing NOT to do when you meet a BLE is sell to them. They are not interested in your products and services or solutions that you can offer. BLEs spend less than 2% of their time with vendors. Boiler plate presentations setting out what you do will not be interesting and you will simply get directed to other more junior people in the organisation.

Board level executives don't get up in the morning thinking about interacting with their professional advisers. They are more likely to be focused on the challenges facing their business, such as improving sales and bottom line profitability, working on strategies that will help them to grow the business, expand market share, remain competitive, manage risk, retain good staff, acquire new customers, and improve workforce productivity. So, you MUST be able to engage with a BLE on their agenda and help them to address their priorities.

| Critical knowledge | Sources |
|---|---|
| • Overall business strategy.<br>• Potential problems and opportunities (theirs not yours).<br>• Most urgent problems and priorities for the business.<br>• Implications for the business of not solving them or addressing the challenges.<br>• Potential pay offs. | **Information** – analyst reports, analyst conference calls, web-based intelligence reports, reports from the various horizon scanning activities.<br><br>**People** – intermediaries, your contacts, external advisers, competitors. |

Proprietary research and other sources of thought leadership are a great way to engage with board level executives in a way that will create value for them. However, if this is going to be the basis of your C-suite engagement strategy, you need to consider the following:

- Position yourself as an adviser and point them in the direction of things they should be thinking about and why;
- Understand your client's organisational challenges, to optimise your use of thought leadership;
- Avoid "me–too" use of thought leadership (this is where a piece of proprietary research can be helpful);
- Offer ideas and perspectives not previously thought of – be a teacher;
- Be disruptive;
- CREATE value not COMMUNICATE value.

**Summary of what you have learnt in this chapter**

- Who you know and are engaging with is a real source of competitive advantage;
- More people involved in decision-making – you are now dealing with buying groups;
- 7 types of buyer with different drivers and you need to deal with each one differently;
- Understand who has the power and who is aligned to you – and who are your competitors talking to
- Use your understanding of power and alignment to create a stake-holder map – and plan your account navigation strategy to enhance your influence and competitive advantage;
- The C-Suite now more involved in scrutinising the decisions of others;
- Use thought leadership as the basis of your engagement strategy with the C-Suite;
- A lot of organisations have a formal approach to procurement – understanding how procurement works in your client organisation and engaging with the procurement team is essential. Don't keep them at arm's length.

# Chapter 10

## Winning with procurement – how to drive most value out of your partnership with procurement

No chapter about understanding who makes decisions, influencing the right people and stakeholder management would be complete without a section on dealing with procurement. At one time the cost of financial advice, consultancy services, the audit, legal advice etc. was seen as a cost of doing business. While the procurement team has been involved in buying goods and other outsourced services for a long time, professional advice has largely been left alone. However, this is no longer the case and now that the procurement team's influence has extended to cover professional services, sellers need to know how to deal effectively with members of the procurement team. Ignoring the procurement team or relying on the assumption that there is nothing you can do to influence procurement are not effective strategies.

The table below illustrates the effectiveness of three different engagement strategies in winning new contracts. As this shows, the most effective strategy for engaging with the procurement team is one of collaboration. If you spend time getting to know the members of the procurement team and understand their objectives and what they are seeking to achieve, you will have much greater influence than if you ignore them.

fig 19. Procuremnet engagement strategies

Source: Huthwaite International

Historically, there has always been tension between members of the procurement team and stakeholders in the business. One of the unique characteristics in selecting professional advisers and buying professional services, is the importance of the relationship between stakeholders in the business and individual people in professional firms – in short people buy people and for that reason, the normal terms of engagement that procurement expect to have with other suppliers of goods and services, don't apply. The people in the business who you generally work with day-to-day, such as GCs, members of the finance team, business managers believe they know who it is best to instruct and are responsible for selecting professional advisers and buying specialist professional services. They believe that procurement have a limited understanding of working with lawyers, accountants and other professional advisers and an agenda which is focused solely on reducing cost, which in their view will have a negative impact on the quality of service delivered to the business. Furthermore, stakeholders responsible for selecting professional advisers are generally quite senior in their organisation (GC, CFO, COO, director level) and may well have worked in practice earlier in their career, before moving in-house. Consequently, they often have long-standing relationships and very strong views on which suppliers they want to work with, based on previous experiences and strenuously resist, what they regard as interference

There was a time when procurement was largely an administrative function with responsibility for managing the process and whose focus was largely driving down costs. Their ability to engage and influence senior stakeholders was limited and procurement was marginalised from the selection of professional advisers. Furthermore, suppliers were very astute at utilising their relationships with stakeholders to bypass procurement and reduce procurement's influence on the sourcing process.

In many cases, this is still true. There are very few professional services category specialists and where this is the case, it makes dealing with procurement very difficult because as with other goods and services they buy, members of the procurement team simply want to drive down price.

However, in many organisations, this is no longer the case. Procurement teams are much more experienced at sourcing professional services and significantly better at engaging internally with stakeholders and demonstrating their value to the business. In most businesses where there is a mature procurement function, members of the procurement team work with their colleagues and collaborate together in selecting and managing professional advisers. The tensions have largely disappeared, procurement recognises the importance of the relationship.

Whatever the status of procurement in your clients' organisation, ignoring procurement is no longer an appropriate strategy.

Many organisations such as the public sector, pharmaceutical, health trusts, insurance companies, banking, manufacturing, retail, utilities and infrastructure have well-established and mature procurement functions. The head of procurement often has a seat on the board and, if not a member of the C-suite will be a member of the senior leadership team. Within these established procurement departments there will be a number of "category specialists" who have responsibility for the procurement of certain types of goods and services e.g. IT and technology, construction and property, clinical services etc.

Many organisations now have category specialists who assist in the sourcing and supplier management of the organisation's professional advisers. For example, the Royal Mail had, within their procurement team, a former lawyer. Her job was to engage with the GC, members of the legal team and other stakeholders in the business to advise and work with them on the selection and ongoing management of their external legal advisers so that the business got the best possible value.

Her priorities included paying the right fee for the job (this varied according to the naturee of the work, whether it was "business critical" or low complexity), using the right performance indicators, ensuring appropriate management information was available. She was widely respected by stakeholders throughout the business and her advice on sourcing and supplier management was frequently sought.

**Developing your strategy for engaging with procurement**

Your strategy for engaging with procurement and gaining influence begins with assessing the maturity of procurement within the organisation you are selling to. If it is an existing client you are looking to develop, then your procurement engagement strategy forms an important part of your client development plan.

There are three levels of maturity of procurement that you need to recognise and they are:

- Immature
- Progressive
- Mature

Each level of maturity has very clear lead indicators, which is the information you need to plan your engagement strategy. Set out below is a table of the eight lead indicators you need to assess the maturity of procurement in any organisation.

| Lead indicator | Immature | Progressive | Mature |
|---|---|---|---|
| Perception of procurement and their relationship with other stakeholders | Not valued by stakeholders in the business and viewed as an administrative function | Recognised as guardian of the process but nothing more | Procurement is well respected by other stakeholders in the business |
| Stage in the buying process when procurement are involved | Only involved at the end when other stakeholders have defined their requirements | Procurement help source but other stakeholders specify | Engaged early as part of a cross functional team with key stakeholders to specify requirements |
| Does the procurement team have dedicated category specialists? | No evidence of category specialists. Individuals source a range of goods and services | Some category specialisation across broad areas e.g. facilities management | Specialist category managers with in-depth knowledge on one area |
| Level of internal compliance with procurement e.g. how much "off panel" work is there? | Poor internal compliance with preferred supplier lists/panels | Still a lot of non - compliance | Majority of spend goes to approved suppliers . |
| How is the procurement team measured by the business? | Measured on the savings they make on purchased goods and services | Broader range of measures beyond price e.g. internal client and employee satisfaction surveys | Targeted to improved total cost savings not just drive down price. Considers cost and value |
| How are procurement involved in ongoing supplier management? | Not involved post purchase in ongoing evaluation | No formal supplier management system. Some supplier reviews | Procurement lead on performance management with tools such as balanced scorecards and quarterly reviews |
| Organisational structure of procurement | Decentralised and fragmented and individuals may have other roles | Procurement more recognisable as a business function | Centralised buying organisation |
| Reporting structure - where does procurement report to? | Head of procurement reports to COO or CFO 2 or 3 levels below board | No place on the board. Head of procurement usually reports to CFO | Seat on the board |

fig 20. Procurement maturity framework

If the procurement function is "immature", the likelihood is that you can largely ignore them. In this case the procurement team's responsibility is probably to provide administrative support to the business and their involvement won't extend beyond managing the procurement process. So, making sure you meet the required deadlines for returning documents etc. and getting answers to administrative details is the most involvement you'll need to have.

On the other hand, if the procurement function is mature, as it is in many banks, health organisations, public sector bodies, insurance companies and other large corporate and institutional bodies, you need to be smarter. You need to develop the appropriate engagement strategy to ensure you have the right influence. Remember in this situation, there is every likelihood that key stakeholders are taking the advice and being guided by members of the procurement team. Where procurement is mature, they have influence. Stakeholders throughout the business respect and value the involvement of the procurement team in making major business decisions and so it is important that you engage with procurement early in the buying journey and align yourself to their objectives and priorities.

## Five tactics for dealing with procurement

Throughout this book I have provided practical tips to improve sales effectiveness, so in the final part of this chapter, I want to give you some tactics to use with procurement.

1. **Procurement tactic – attempts to discredit your value proposition**

   The procurement team's tactic is to undermine the value you have built up with stakeholders in the business, so that they can simply use price to compare you with other suppliers. Your tactic, therefore, should be to focus on stakeholders in the business to develop a strong business case and a clear demonstration of value. Work with stakeholders who have influence – they can either ignore their colleagues in procurement or successfully sell you to procurement.

2. **Procurement tactic – commoditise and control the process**

   Procurement like to control every aspect of the sale and like to do apples–apples comparisons and evaluation of suppliers against their prescribed list of criteria. However, with professional services it is rare that all the apples are the same. Your tactic is to adopt a value based selling approach focused on how you will help your client achieve their goals. As with the previous tactic, concentrate on engaging with key stakeholders in the business.

3. **Procurement tactic – limit access to the business**

   As we have discussed previously, procurement like to control all aspects of the sales process, including who you speak to. They want to limit the risk of being surprised by a stakeholder in the business making a decision that undermines or overrides the procurement process. Procurement generally hate surprises or to feel they are not in control. Not surprisingly you can count this tactic by having strong networks and influence with key stakeholders in the business. The earlier in the sales process you can be exploring and influencing your clients' needs the better, before procurement put a gagging order on suppliers. If you are told you can't speak to anyone outside the RFP process, you have to make a judgement in terms of the risks and rewards of complying. If you have strong relationships with key stakeholders in the business, it is highly unlikely you will be disqualified. However, if you have been invited to tender and you don't have strong relationships with key stakeholders in the business, you should seriously consider your chances of success.

4. **Procurement tactic – use history or past performance against you**
   Procurement always like to have as much ammunition as possible to use against suppliers to drive down price and negotiate a "commodity deal", so it is important to anticipate any concerns and have your responses ready. Again, focus on value and support your proposal with evidence.

5. **Procurement tactic – last minute hoops and changes to the sales process**
   As we have already touched on, procurement like to be in control and keep the power on their side and they are very good a letting suppliers believe that they have all the power. One of the tactics they use is to introduce additional decision-makers and other hoops to jump through – late in the process. This puts pressure on suppliers which can improve the terms they agree with procurement. Therefore it is important to work hard during the scoping phase to find out everyone who will be involved in making, influencing or scrutinising the decision. You also need to know HOW the decision will be made – the decision criteria (DC), timeline, key stages, internal processes etc. this makes it difficult to simply introduce, without explanation, additional steps to go through or decision-makers to satisfy.

**Summary of what you have learnt in this chapter**

1. Engage and align yourself with procurement. Collaborate where possible and work together.
2. Don't leave it too late. As with other stakeholders, if you wait until the invitation to tender arises, your influence will be limited and may only extend to discussions on fees and other terms of engagement.
3. Understand the role of procurement in your clients' organisations – are they simply an administrative function, managing a process, or are they strategic advisers to the business on the selection of professional advisers and ongoing supplier management?
4. Understand the procurement team's drivers – they may well be different to other stakeholders in the business.
5. Recognise the negotiation tactics of the procurement team. The following are common examples of tactics used by procurement at any point in the client's buying journey and you need to resist early attempts to negotiate fees.

*"We expect all our suppliers to discount their fees by x"*

*"You are more expensive than your competitors"*

*"What discounts are you prepared to offer?"*

At the very least you should not give anything away without trading something in return e.g. volume of work, length of contract etc.

# Chapter 11

## Pitch up to win

You've gotten to know your client, you've met various stakeholders, you know their needs and they've learnt more about you and your firm. You may have been through an initial shortlisting exercise. However, there is still the question why should a prospect or client pick you and your firm to work with rather than one of your competitors? Let's face it, most professional firms offer similar technical capability and a similar range of services. Of course, we all think we have something unique – cheaper fees, better market intelligence, and a bigger team of industry specialists. But the reality is that, in the eyes of buyers, there is very little difference between competing firms and so they use other factors to influence and make decisions.

The sales process may be long and complex and will involve many meetings with a variety of people in the client organisation, frequent exchanges of emails, delivery of information at various points and the client may indicate you are the preferred supplier. Yet, at the end of the day, it is frequently the firm that delivers the most compelling sales presentation that actually wins the business.

Whatever the format, of your sales presentation – be it formal or informal, it plays a critical role in influencing your client or prospect's decision and will often determine whether they buy from you or one of your competitors. In this chapter I want to look at some practical tips and techniques that will increase the persuasive power of your sales presentations.

There are a number of common traps that teams and individuals fall into when making sales presentations, which I want to help you avoid or overcome:

- Too many presentations focus on the seller's capabilities and the features of their firm, and not the client's needs;
- Solutions are not sufficiently tailored to the client's needs;
- Don't answer the "why us?" question;
- Attempts by sellers to differentiate themselves are often not relevant to the client and they fail to provide the evidence;
- In many cases the value of the solution is less than the cost – as the client sees it;
- The presentation is poorly structured and so it is difficult to understand;
- Lack of preparation by the presenters;
- Poor teamwork in the presentation.

A powerful and persuasive presentation that stands out from your competitors needs to focus on two critical factors in equal measure:

- Content
- Delivery

The sales presentation is a crucial step in the sales process and is often the only opportunity to influence all the decision-makers. If the sales presentation is poorly delivered and the content is not memorable, all the previous good work that has gone on in the earlier stages of the sales process will be lost.

For clients, the presentation may be just one of several they sit through during the day. If the team is going to beat the competitors, they and their presentation need to be persuasive and memorable.

Most presentation skills courses focus on **how you say it** rather than on **what you say.** This is important for improving a presenter's performance, so that they come across as enthusiastic, professional and memorable. However, this does little to ensure the content is persuasive and powerful, and this is equally important in a sales presentation.

Set out below is an illustration of what sellers need to concentrate on to maximise the persuasive power of their presentation.

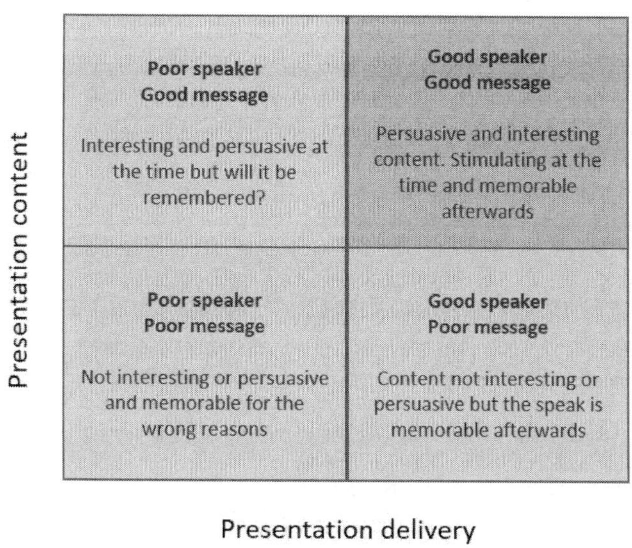


fig 21. Content v delivery

As the table shows, even the best prepared case can fail to make an impact if it is poorly delivered and the most polished presenters will fail to get the outcome they want if the content isn't convincing – though the speakers may emerge with their credibility intact or even enhanced.

So, the message is clear, "what you say" in sales presentations is equally important as "how you say it". Therefore, how can you ensure that you deliver presentations and have the greatest chance of winning the business?

## Persuasive content

A persuasive and powerful presentation is interesting, relevant, easy to follow, easy to understand and demonstrates a strong value proposition.

There are **six** golden rules to follow, that will ensure you achieve this:

- **Structure the presentation** – to make the sequence of your presentation and your overall approach clear;
- **Use signposting** – to lead the audience through the presentation and make it easy to follow;
- **Make it relevant to the needs of the audience** – which makes your presentation convincing and meaningful;
- **Use illustrations** – to make it interesting, easy to understand and appear both informative and detailed;
- **Provide "social proof"** – to demonstrate success;
- **Support your presentation with visual aids** – 40% of people respond better and have higher recall if information is presented visually.

## Provide a road map for your audience

You need to make it easy for your audience to follow your presentation and avoid getting confused and lost. If they can't follow the presentation easily they will quickly disengage and the persuasive power of your presentation is lost! Let's look at a few guidelines to follow that will enable you to deliver a well-structured presentation that is easy to follow.

As everyone knows, all good presentations have a beginning, a middle and an end. Another way of describing the overall structure is to say what you are going to say, say it and then say what you've said.

**Begin your presentation**

The overall purpose of the opening part of your presentation is to manage the expectations of the audience, and should include:

- The overall purpose of the presentation
- Timing
- Introductions (if necessary)
- Key topics you intend to cover
- How you will deal with questions
- Note-taking

The opening part of your presentation will only be a few minutes and then you can move onto the main body of what you want to talk about. Here's an example which covers the main points required for the opening. It's important that you sound authentic, so find a style that works for you.

*"Good afternoon and many thanks for inviting us to this presentation. We know you are looking to appoint estate managers and in our presentation we aim to show you how we can help you achieve you goals over the next five years. Our presentation will last around 30 minutes after which we are happy to answer any questions. I am joined today by Elaine Thomas, who will talk about how we will review you property portfolio, I will talk to you about project management and my colleague Andrew James will cover you planning requirements. We have an information pack we'll leave with you but please take any notes you feel are relevant. I'd like to start by asking ..."*

## Get into the detail

Now you can move on to the main body of your presentation. There are essentially 2 types of presentation:

- Information – providing information and briefing for an audience
- Persuasion – to motivate the audience to act

Too often sales presentations inform rather than persuade and so the team fails to win the business. How you structure the body of your presentation will have a material impact on its persuasive power.

Talk about **them** first, not about you. First and foremost, the audience is interested in whether you understand what they want and how you can help. Set out below is a suggested structure for the main part of your presentation.

**Structuring a sales presentation**

**Opening**

- Purpose, timing, introductions, key topics, note-taking, dealing with questions etc.

**Main body of the sales presentation**

- Client requirements and priorities;
- Other issues/considerations, thought leadership, insights etc. – tell them something relevant that they don't know;
- Your solutions;
- Pay off for the clients – i.e. how they will be better off?
- Why us – addressing decision criteria?
- Implementation – if appropriate;
- Key facts about the firm e.g. who will be in the team, who else they work for, firm history (if appropriate);
- Fees – yes, at the end so that you can build the value for what you can do before you talk about cost.

**Closing**

- Summarise what you have talked about;
- Reinforce key messages;
- Call to action;
- Invite questions.

## Guide your audience through the presentation

In a 20- or 30-minute sales presentation you may well cover a number of topics and provide significant amounts of information. You need to be certain that you take the audience with you through the presentation.

There are four very useful techniques to help you do this.

- Signposting – essentially tells the audience you have reached a crossroads in your presentation and gives them the new direction.

*"So, that's all I need to say on that point and now I'd like to move on to talk about how we predict currency fluctuations, which was another of your priorities".*

... moving on we come to the final point

The next point I want to cover is...

Signposting can also be used to introduce another speaker and set the agenda for what they are going to talk about.

*"That's all I'm going to say, and I now want to hand you over to Andrew, who will talk about transaction management and optimising efficiency".*

## Utility statements

These are statements that flag to the audience what you are about to cover and why it is important. This is a valuable technique for when you want to focus the audience on the key messages you want them to remember.

You can plan them into your presentations and if not over-used can be very powerful

To help you make a decision, I will describe 2 options

To help you assess the value of this approach to project management, I'd like to set out a short case study

- Summarising

Summarising helps to reinforce key messages either at key points in your presentation or at the end. The summary at the end of your presentation is particularly important as it enables you to emphasise the key takeaway messages from your presentation.

*In the last few minutes, I've covered forecasting, timing and measurement, so now I want to move on to address the final point you asked us to talk to you about".*

So far we have come to the following conclusions, which I'd like to remind us of before we move on...

Effective summaries are concise, accurate and do not introduce new information.

- Linking

As the term suggests, linking is concerned with referencing other parts of your presentation. It may be used to refer back to something you or a colleague has already said, or to forward reference something you will be speaking about. Linking helps to make your presentation coherent, reinforces major points, pre-empts questions, strengthens the overall structure and enhances credibility.

Linking is particularly important in longer presentations where there may be a number of speakers, to increase clarity and understanding.

## The impact of structuring on your audience

The Huthwaite Research group observed a number of sales presentations and they discovered a material difference in the impact of a presentation on an audience depending on the amount of structuring:

When there were high levels of structuring, the audience described the presentations as:

- Organised
- Tight
- Clear
- Methodical
- Efficient
- Well planned

When there were low levels of structuring the audience described presentations as:

- Loose
- Inefficient
- Time wasting
- Hard to listen to

## Relating your presentation to the needs of the audience

The audience's main questions, in any sales presentation, are *"do these people understand our needs and priorities?"* and *"does their solution address our needs and priorities?"* So, if you ensure the content relates directly to the needs, concerns and priorities of your audience, your presentation will be highly relevant and powerful. A word of warning, when I talk about relating a presentation to client needs, I mean the needs they have explicitly told you about. As an expert in your field, it is too easy to make assumptions about your clients' needs.

Your presentation must also clearly demonstrate the gains and how a client will be better off if they use you. In essence, you need to show how you can help, not just focus on what you do.

Clients don't wake up in the morning thinking about what products or services they want to buy. They are concerned about their margins, profitability, what risks the business is facing, protecting reputation, and how they can reduce costs and improve efficiencies and so on. So, make sure you address their concerns and focus your presentation on their agenda.

**How will you ensure successful implementation?**

Finally, when thinking about how to relate your presentation to the needs of the audience, there is another question that you need to address. At some point the audience will also ask *"can we make this work for us?", "are there any risks?", "what are the pitfalls for us if we use this firm?", so* your presentation should also clearly address any concerns the client may have in relation to implementation.

**A case in point...**

A large telecoms company wanted to appoint a new firm of lawyers to handle their employment work. Traditionally the in-house legal team had either done the employment work themselves or, if they had capacity or capability problems, they instructed a variety of external organisations with whom they worked.

At the time of the presentation, the management team were experiencing some resistance to appointing one firm to the panel for employment work, and they had flagged this up in the meetings prior to the pitch.

The presentation team addressed this issue in their presentation. In the feedback after the presentation the client admitted that there had been a real possibility they would have stuck with the status quo, if the team hadn't addressed the issue, as the proposed change was proving too difficult.

## Include relevant thought leadership in your presentation

Addressing the client's needs in your presentation is your number 1 priority, but clients are always interested in what else they should be thinking about, or what other organisations in their sector are doing. Your presentation should also include some relevant thought leadership or market insight, which will give you the opportunity to provide an opinion or a new perspective on something. Effective use of relevant thought leadership and insights is a great way to improve the persuasive power of your presentation.

## Why choose us?

The final question you need to answer is *"why us"*. However formal or informal the sales presentation is, there are always competitors that the client is considering – and this might be an internal resource.

In order to evaluate and compare competing suppliers, a client will use a set of decision criteria (DC). Hopefully in the meetings prior to the pitch, you will have discovered or even influenced the decision criteria the client will use.

In your presentation you need to demonstrate how you meet the client's decision criteria and how you meet them better than competitors do.

We looked in detail at decision criteria in chapter 4 so let's remind ourselves about what they are and how clients use them.

- The decision criteria clients typically use include details such as responsiveness, accessibility, sector knowledge, price, team resources, sector knowledge and of course do they like you and can they work with you;
- Decision criteria don't typically include technical capability or track record – it's generally accepted that if you have been asked to make a presentation, the client is happy you have the necessary expertise;
- Not all decision criteria are of equal importance to a client;
- Different stakeholders involved in the decision may have different priorities with regards to DCs;
- In more formal pitches – often those led by procurement – clients will be very transparent about what their decision criteria are and how they are weighted;
- Clients use DCs to compare suppliers.

You need to uncover the client's DCs and their relative importance, then in the presentation show how you meet them and meet them better than your competitors. Decision criteria are the basis of your competitive advantage. The earlier in the sales process that you can talk to clients about their DCs, the better, and of course you then have the opportunity to introduce criteria they may not have thought of, but where you are strong.

**A case in point...**

I was working with a client who had developed a piece of project management software which enabled clients doing major transactions, to run them more efficiently. This meant they were often able to complete more quickly, there were less "hitches" along the way, fewer aborted transactions, and costs were significantly reduced. Where appropriate, my client encouraged their clients to specify availability of project management software as one of their decision criteria, as this gave them a strong competitive advantage.

## Enhancing the content of your presentation

Using examples, stories and social proof help to bring your presentation alive, makes it easier to understand and more interesting for the audience to listen to. It also helps to build credibility. We refer to the use of these techniques in a presentation as **Elaboration** and there is a direct correlation between the amount of elaboration you use and its persuasive power as you will see later in the chapter.

Any example or story you use must be relevant to the audience; it should not be too long and must be simple to understand.

*"As a third-party buying organisation our fees are generally related to the savings we make for you – let me show you how this would work".*

*"Using our project management software will enable you to be more efficient – for example..."*

Telling a story in a presentation can enhance it in a number of ways:

- It makes your presentation more memorable – concepts or facts that are wrapped up in a story, are 20 times more memorable than just plain facts.
- Puts the audience's ego to sleep – a story may challenge the clients thinking without the client thinking you are challenging them and feeling they are under attack. A story simply presents a scenario that allows the client to draw their own conclusions. It makes your message easier to receive.
- Facts and figures are often too abstract, and the audience may not feel they affect them. A story helps to make sense of what is otherwise abstract.
- Fills the audience's knowledge gap – which enhances your value and credibility particularly if your story or word picture gets them thinking about something they had not previously thought about or considered important.

**A case in point...**

In a recent presentation, I talked about the importance of having a detailed picture and understanding of a client's stakeholder network and the risk of losing out to competitors, if you do not. *(theoretical and conceptual on its own).*

I illustrated this with a story from one of my law firm clients. My client was pitching for the legal work for one of the large utility companies. They had very good relationships with stakeholders in the company's legal team as well as stakeholders in the various divisions. All their contacts were in the middle management tier. My concern was that the decision to change lawyers is a significant decision and not without its risks for the company. I felt that there may be involvement and scrutiny elsewhere in the business and possibly even at board level. I felt we should map the stakeholders and ask 2 questions:

- Do we know all the people we need to know?
- Who are our competitors talking to that we are not?
- What is our stakeholder navigation strategy to ensure we are well positioned to win?

In the end the company stayed put with their existing lawyers because the FD and the CEO knew them better!

Finally, I want to talk about the importance of using **Social Proof** to enhance your pitch. Proof statements based directly on third-party experiences can add credibility to your business case and therefore the persuasive power of your presentation. The key, of course, is to select an organisation that is relevant and recognised as credible to the audience. You also need to be confident that the organisation you use in your proof statement will verify your claims.

*"Benjie LLP have used our project management software and over the last 3 years, they tell us they have reduced costs by 10–15%".*

*"Broadhursts adopted our approach to bid management and their win rate has increased by 15%".*

Interestingly, 70% of executive buyers in Gartner's buyer survey said that the best way for individuals or teams to deliver differentiation, that they trust, is by sharing a customer story.

The Huthwaite Research group established that where presentations include significant numbers of examples, stories and proof statements – Elaboration – the audience describe presentations as **detailed, informative**, and **comprehensive.** Where the levels are low, audiences describe presentations as **incomplete, too abstract, uninformative** and **incomplete.**

## Visual aids should support your presentation, not lead it

*"A picture paints a thousand words"– Fred R. Barnard*

A presentation supported by visual aids will be more memorable and easier for the audience to recall. We process visual information 60,000 times faster than text, and as I said earlier in this chapter, 40% of people respond better and have higher recall if information is presented visually. However, there are some guiding principles:

- Visual aids are not a speaker prop to be used as a substitute for inadequate preparation;
- They are there to enhance your presentation for the audience;
- Visual aids (in whatever format you use them) should emphasise key messages, illustrate facts and key concepts to make your presentation less abstract;
- Where possible, try to use illustrations rather than text e.g. graphs, charts, photo and video clips, cartoons (where appropriate).

Finally, the attention of the audience should focus on you and your presentation, not your PowerPoint slides – their purpose is to add impact to your presentation not to be the presentation.

## Make your presentation memorable

At the start of this chapter, I said that a powerful and persuasive presentation that stands out from your competitors needs to focus on both persuasive content and memorable delivery.

So far, we have looked at persuasive content. Now I want to turn your attention to delivery. Nothing I'm going to say in this part of the chapter will be new, but I want to remind you of a few key principles.

Whatever your style of delivery and whatever techniques you use, it is important that style does not overpower substance. There is a delicate balance to be struck – solid content but weak delivery is as bad as excellent delivery but a lack of substance.

Deliver your presentation with confidence and passion. Passionate people have influence and people want to listen to them. An audience is more likely to believe and be persuaded by you if you are confident and passionate in how you speak to them. Of course, confidence and passion is not something you can buy in a bottle and drink before a presentation, it comes with practice and approaching presentations with a positive mind set. Part of your preparation – which we'll move onto later in the chapter – is ensuring you have positive dialogues going on in your head as you approach your presentation.

Vary the pace, volume and intonation of your voice. This will help the audience to stay engaged and listening to your presentation. Uncomfortable though it may be, a useful exercise is to record your presentation and then listen back to see how well you use your voice. Your voice can be very useful for emphasising key messages particularly when accompanied by silences to let those messages sink in.

There are also some verbal techniques that will help you to emphasise the key points you want the audience to remember:

- **Rhetorical questions** – These are not questions that you intend the audience to answer. Their purpose is to engage with the audience and grab their attention. If you use rhetorical questions tactically they can add impact at key points of your presentation. Part of your preparation could be to read through your presentation and identify key points at which you really want to hook the audience and drop in rhetorical questions.

- **Repetition and emphasis** – Verbal repetition used with non-verbal repetition will help you to emphasise key messages and ensure the audience remembers them. *Repetition* is the simple *repeating* of a *word*, within a short space of words. Repetition draws the attention of the audience to key points and increases memorability.

*"With this approach you will save time, save money and save effort"*

As with rhetorical questions, it is a good idea to review your presentation, identify messages you want the audience to remember and decide how you can stress their importance to ensure your message really hits home.

*"If there is one thing you take away today, let it be this..."*

*"The most important point I'd like to leave you with is..."*

*"The next three points are critical to your success, I believe."*

## Handling a low reacting audience

Audience behaviour and how you perceive they are responding to your presentation, can have a material effect on you as a presenter and the success of your presentation. One type of audience behaviour that is uncomfortable and unsettling, is "low reacting". Individuals who are described as 'low reactors', reveal very little about whether they agree or disagree with what you are saying. This will leave you feeling uncertain and you may begin to feel stressed. A lot of professional buyers such as procurement people use low reacting as a pressure tactic, so it's important you recognise this behaviour and know what to do.

The impact of a low reacting audience on an unsuspecting presenter is a feeling that you are losing control, and this may lead you to:

- Speak too quickly;
- Lose your voice;
- Lose the presentation sequence as you try to find something to say that will impress them;
- Exaggerate arguments without using good supporting evidence;
- Not ask questions or engage non-verbally because of the lack of rewarding response.

There are, however, some tactics you can use to deal with this challenging behaviour.

As part of your preparation, anticipate who may be low reactors – senior buyers, procurement.

- Be well prepared so that low reaction doesn't knock your confidence;
- Seek the reaction of specific people, who are not reacting, by asking questions and testing understanding;

*"Can I just check, is that something you agree with?"*

*"Have I explained that, is there anything you'd like to me to go over again?"*

- Express feelings;

*"I'm getting a sense that I might have confused you, would you like me to explain again?"*

*"You look as though you might disagree, is that right?"*

Dealing confidently with these behaviours will help you to maintain control. It's also important to remember that you are in the spotlight during your presentation. The audience will see how you handle difficult behaviour, which will affect your credibility and the response of the audience – for good or bad!

**Summary of what you have learnt in this chapter**

- **A powerful and persuasive presentation** that stands out from your competitors, needs to focus on two critical factors in equal measure – content and delivery. You need to balance style and substance.
- **Your presentation should have a clear beginning, middle and end.**
- **Provide a roadmap for your audience** to guide them through the presentation and make it easy to follow. Techniques such as sign-posting, summarising, utility statements and linking statements will help.
- **Make sure your presentation meets the needs of your audience –** their needs, not your assumptions.
- **Use Elaboration techniques to enhance your presentation and make it more persuasive –** stories, illustrations, examples and remember the impact of social proof to reassure the audience.
- **Use relevant thought leadership and insights –** to deliver value and build your credibility.
- **Deliver your presentation with confidence and passion –** to ensure it stands out from the competition and the audience remembers it.
- **Emphasise key points and important messages** using rhetorical questions and repetition.
- **Recognise and learn to deal with low reacting audiences.**
- **PREPARE, PREPARE, PREPARE.**

# KEEP IT

# Chapter 12

## On-boarding new clients to optimise revenue and retention

Congratulations! You've been pursuing a really exciting new client for the last few months. You and your colleagues have had numerous meetings and spent hours discussing your proposal and at last you've won the client. It's tempting, at this point to take your foot off the gas and bask in your success. In reality, this is where the hard work needs to start if you are to maximise the return on all your investment of time and effort. Having won a new client, you need to manage the on-boarding of that client as robustly and proactively as you managed the sales process. On-boarding is, in fact, the final stage in the sales process and ensures you can successfully embed the relationship and optimise the revenue.

The acquisition and on-boarding of new clients are two of the biggest challenges faced by professional firms. All firms recognise the importance of resourcing business development, however, while much hard work and effort and resource go into client acquisition, the subsequent on-boarding of a new client can often fall by the wayside. This is not surprising since so many of the performance measures and metrics are related to winning new clients. There are often more bells rung and whistles blown when the firm wins a new client than there is for the growth and retention of existing clients. So often a huge amount of resources go into winning new clients – both human and monetary resource – then when the client is won. After the initial euphoria and "phew we did it!", there can be a tendency to sit back and wait for the instructions to come in. I see this particularly with panel appointments or appointments to preferred supplier lists. In the absence of a clear and well-executed on-boarding strategy, the risk is the instructions simply won't come, going instead to competitors, who may be better known or have stronger relationships with key stakeholders.

Frequently, a firm's appointment to a panel or supplier list or for a particular transaction, is seen as the end of the process. However, the opposite is in fact true; it is the beginning of a journey for you and the client, and is a journey which the client team needs to manage.

In this chapter I am going to explore what is meant by on-boarding new clients, why it's important and set out a simple but rigorous approach to ensure you maximise the revenue, accelerate the growth, reduce the risk of defection and ensure the long-term loyalty and retention of clients.

## So what do we mean when we talk about on-boarding clients?

On-boarding, as we have already stated, is the final stage in the sales process. It's the strategy you implement immediately after you have been appointed, to ensure the client's experience and their journey with you is positive, meets their expectations (and more) and enables them to achieve their goals and aspirations. Rapid growth and successful retention of a new client means you don't leave the initial stages of engagement to chance. The successful on-boarding of a new client means being proactive and rigorous in how you get to know the client (including addressing any residual concerns that may have come up in the sales process), managing the client's expectations, aligning the two businesses and most importantly making it easy for the client to work with you and do business. Harvard Business Review reported that the single most effective way to build loyalty and retention is "to make it easy". The study identified three steps to create a positive client experience:

- **Remove obstacles** – eliminate anything that stands in the way of the client having a straightforward experience of working with you.
- **Agree how you will communicate**.
- **Assign responsibilities** both to the client and internally, to ensure you deliver what the client expects and show that you are straightforward to do business with.
- **Listen to your clients** – communicate effectively with clients and work effectively internally with team members to meet your client's expectations and to ensure no stone is left unturned in helping clients to meet their goals.
- **Use feedback to improve the client's experience** – check in regularly with clients and make questionnaires and review meetings an integral part of your service delivery.
- **A rigorous framework and approach** to on-boarding new clients is critical but it needs to be balanced with a tailored approach as one size does not fit all. Later in this chapter we'll look at the framework of activities you need to undertake to successfully on-board new clients.

## The importance of on-boarding new clients and the risks of not doing so

A successful on-boarding strategy ensures you exceed client expectations, optimise revenues, accelerate growth and build a long-term, mutually beneficial and sustainable relationship, which extends the client lifetime value. However, in many cases, on-boarding is an afterthought rather than a strategic relationship-building opportunity. Advisers and their team move onto the next new client they want to pursue rather than working on creating a lasting relationship with the client they have just won.

When new clients are on-boarded successfully as part of a well-defined and organised client management strategy, the results are predictable:

- Client trust develops faster and is stronger
- Levels of engagement with the client is higher
- The long-term client–adviser bond is deeper
- The client sees the value of partnership
- Clients are more likely to become advocates
- Greater competitive advantage

Research shows that the first 90 days after acquiring a new client, is critical. According to Ricardo Craft, senior Vice President at ServiceSource, if a client doesn't become loyal within 90 days of appointment, then there's typically only a 10% chance they ever will.

*"Hold your client's hand for 90 days and they'll be loyal for life"*
*– John Jantsch, Author*

Successful on-boarding of a new client enables you to optimise the revenue, accelerate growth and retain the client. Management consultants Bain & Co reported that a 5% increase in client retention can boost profits by up to 95%. Much of this increase in profits comes from the fact it costs between 10 and 20 times more to win new clients than it does to retain and grow existing clients. The cost of winning business has increased dramatically in recent years so holding onto and growing existing clients has to be a key part of the sales strategy in any professional firm. Neglecting this important step in nurturing new clients can be costly in terms of revenue, client retention and the potential for referrals.

Before we move on to what you need to include in your on-boarding strategy, let me just say that there will be many new client wins that don't justify this level of investment. That's not to say they don't require high levels of service excellence, but that may not extend to implementing a detailed on-boarding strategy.

## Mapping the first 100 days – planning your on-boarding strategy

As I have already highlighted, the first 100 days following your appointment by a new client are critical, in order to build a long-term relationship and optimise revenue and profitability. No one size fits all in terms of your on-boarding strategy and it is important to develop the appropriate approach for each client. However, there are some general principles and these are listed below.

In broad terms the on-boarding strategy is divided into three stages:

- Initiate
- Engage
- Cultivate

The activities you need to think about at each stage are set out in the table below. Use this as a starting place to customising your on-boarding strategy for new clients.

<table>
<tr><td>Initiate</td><td><ul><li>Set the client up on internal systems</li><li>Update CRM system</li><li>Ensure compliance with legislative and regulatory requirements</li><li>Communicate proposed on-boarding plan so that the client knows what to expect</li><li>Assign the client service team</li><li>Brief the client service team and the "back office" team (Accounts, IT, analytics etc)</li><li>Revisit and be familiar with the RFP/ your proposal and any SLA that the client may have given you</li></ul></td><td></td></tr>
<tr><td>Engage</td><td><ul><li>Kick-off meeting① to agree how what was included in your proposal will be delivered and is the start of your operational relationship</li><li>Look for early wins</li><li>Familiarisation meeting, onsite/ client premises②to learn about the client's business, to meet and greet key contacts and others in the business. Demonstrate your knowledge of their business and their sector where relevant.</li><li>Look for early ways to create value e.g. take them to relevant events as a guest, introductions to other people of interest to them in your network</li></ul></td><td>①Finalise contracts and service charter/SLA. Meet key contacts, exchange key information about each other's organisation, identify client's immediate requirements, agree other priorities, and agree time frames, potential roadblocks that may impact the client experience. Agree on how you will work together e.g. communication, billing, KPIs, metrics & reporting, accessing resources. NB focus on making it easy. Swap organisation charts and agree who needs to contact who and about what<br><br>②the value of this activity is 2-fold – to learn more about the client's business but also to show your commitment at an early stage. Be clear you have a detailed understanding of their business, how they do business with their customers and their goals and aspirations</td></tr>
<tr><td>Cultivate</td><td><ul><li>Gather initial client feedback and user experience</li><li>Identify longer term pain points</li><li>Provide early data and analysis</li><li>Prepare client development plan and collaborate with the client on this</li><li>Make changes as needed e.g. client support team, operational changes, reporting, billing etc.</li></ul></td><td></td></tr>
</table>

**Summary of what you have learnt in this chapter**

- **Plan your on-boarding strategy for new clients** – on-boarding new clients is part of your client management strategy and will help you to optimise revenue, accelerate growth, increase retention and build long-term relationships.
- **Don't leave it to chance or let it be an afterthought** – plan your on-boarding strategy and share it with both clients and colleagues.

# Chapter 13

## Client listening – what it is and why it pays!

*"80% of professional firms believe they deliver above average service, only 40% of clients say they do" – Lexis Nexis Bellwether report*

Client listening is the process by which you seek feedback from clients regarding their satisfaction with the services that you provide and is often combined with asking clients about their likely future needs and preferences. The output of listening to clients is that firms then need to apply what they have learnt in how they deliver services in the future. However, despite the simple concept and the benefits to be gained, many firms don't have a rigorous and reliable client listening programme – although if asked most firm leaders would agree that a client listening programme is a worthwhile activity.

In some firms there are pockets of good practice, though much of the feedback is anecdotal and in some firms there is very little attempt to seek feedback at all! Although client listening is much broader than simply taking feedback, the two terms are generally interchangeable.

Everyone working in a professional services firm knows that the client has to be at the centre of everything they do and anything less than a delighted client isn't good enough. Yet, despite this widely held aspiration, many firms fail to engage in a consistent and meaningful way with their clients. Individuals may not see the need, because they believe their clients will tell them if things aren't going well or they may be nervous about engaging with clients on matters beyond the day-to-day management of transactions. Either way, at best, the full value of the relationship is not being exploited or at worst the relationship could be in jeopardy if things that are not going well, are not put right.

Client listening is not new but has only become a systematic and formalised activity relatively recently. Much of the success of individual professional advisers in the past has been because they listened to their clients and looked for ways to improve their service. Those that took the time to seek feedback and listen to their clients were the most successful.

In many firms, client listening is ad hoc and led by those individuals who are sufficiently interested in listening to their clients. Firms often leave it up to individuals to elect whether to engage with their clients and how to do so. While many firms have embraced a more organised and firm-wide approach to client listening and are enjoying the benefits, many have not – often because consultants are over complicating and over specifying what is required.

In this chapter I want to introduce you to the benefits of client listening. I want to present you with a simple yet effective methodology that will help you design, implement and optimise client listening – one that is not onerous or highly resource intensive – that you can easily integrate into your account management activities.

## Client listening – the business imperative?

The cost of winning new clients is up to 20 times more expensive than winning business from existing clients. So, a well-organised and well-executed client listening programme is an extremely important part of any client management programme. It will enable you to listen to clients more systematically and thoroughly and will help to strengthen your ties, build sustainable relationships and win more business.

Let's begin by looking at the levels of client satisfaction in the table below

| | | |
|---|---|---|
| **Zone of Defection** | low levels of satisfaction<br>high levels of dissatisfaction | Clients will switch unless the cost is too high or there are no alternatives. Negative word of mouth promotion. |
| **Zone of Indifference** | intermediate levels of satisfaction | Clients will switch if a better alternative comes along. |
| **Zone of Affection** | very high levels of satisfaction | Clients are fiercely loyal and will praise the firm publicly. Willing and active in making referrals. |

Source:

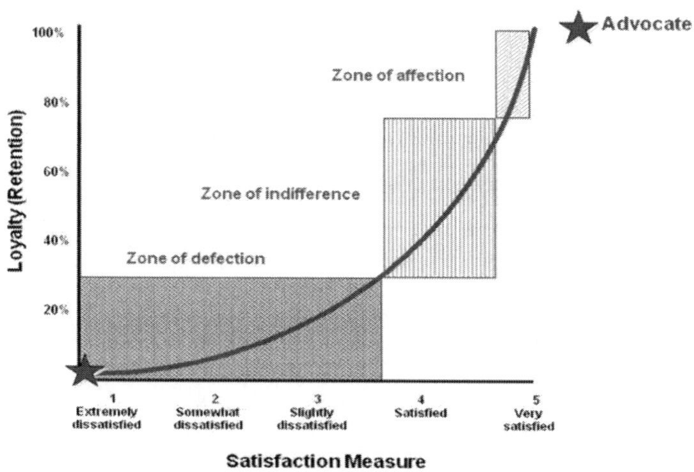


fig. 22. Loyalty & satisfaction graph

Source: Harvard Business Review

Clients that are in the **Zone of Defection** generally make it known. They are forthcoming about the things they are not happy with and their expectations about what needs to change. Some clients may go as far as stating that they are looking at alternatives. Clients in the **Zone of Affection** are also very vocal in their support and their loyalty and they are often very accessible and willing to spend time with you. However, it is the **Zone of Indifference** which is the danger zone. These clients are neither wildly unhappy nor ecstatically happy, therefore they are unlikely to identify themselves to you. You will probably have a good relationship with them. The time you spend with them on work matters will seem constructive, and the time you spend socially will be enjoyable. However, the growth potential of clients in this zone is probably not being fully exploited. You will only know about clients in this zone when they defect because something better has come along – or if you engage with them in a thorough client listening exercise. So, ask yourself – hand on heart – "which of my clients do I know are in the zone of affection?" In all likelihood it will not be many, the majority being in the zone of indifference.

One of the main benefits of client listening is that it helps you get closer to your clients, understand their business better and fully exploit future business opportunities – either with them or the clients they can introduce you too. In simple terms client listening helps to move clients from the zone of defection or zone of indifference to the zone of affection. What's more clients value the chance to provide feedback, as they know that helps them too – in fact, in today's business environment clients expect their professional advisers to want to seek feedback. But it doesn't need to be complicated to enjoy the benefits, as I will show you by the end of this chapter.

Client listening is a means of engaging with clients in a way that is active and productive and helps clients feel valued and involved. It should take both a backward and forward view of the relationship. You need to explore levels of satisfaction with services delivered and also look forward to what is happening in the client's business and in their market or industry group. Running a client listening programme will help you identify issues which may be blocking future progress and that need to be addressed, taking the guess work out of how services need to be delivered now and in the future. It will also help to identify your client's future plans and issues in their industry and allow you to make decisions based on the client's preferences and strategic requirements. Client listening is also a valuable source of competitor intelligence.

## Methodology

There are various ways in which you can undertake client listening, and your choice of which activity to use will be determined by your objectives. The table below sets out a list of the different activities you could use and the pros and cons of each one.

| Method | Advantages | Disadvantages | Uses |
|---|---|---|---|
| Ad hoc | "Checking in" with clients is extremely useful and makes the client feel valued. It is a critical role for client partners and account managers | • inconsistent<br>• irregular<br>• often undocumented<br>• results not shared<br>• clients may hold back<br>• may not cover relevant points | Relationship maintenance |
| Questionnaires | • standardised format<br>• easily delivered to a high volume of respondents<br>• identifies recurring themes introduces consistency to client listening | • no client engagement<br>• does not feel personal<br>• feels boring for the client | Post matter reviews<br><br>Benchmarking service standards<br><br>Tracks consistent service quality around the firm |
| Relationship partner meeting | • demonstrates partners care about the quality of their service<br>• a powerful form of client engagement<br>• often easier to access key stakeholders<br>• can use the opportunity to build the relationship and identify future opportunities<br>• opportunity to other key stakeholders | • time consuming and doesn't get done because of fee earning billable targets etc.<br>• partners may lack the skills to undertake client listening<br>• may avoid awkward issues, be defensive or not "hear" or not report back bad news<br>• may leap to assumptions<br>• clients may hold back too much<br>• client colludes with the partner in the interview *"tell me what you want me to say here"* | Relationship development |
| Managing partner/partner not involved with client meetings | • shows the firm's commitment<br>• can address concerns that couldn't be raised with the relationship partner<br>• may be able to identify cross selling and upselling opportunities<br>• can answer questions about the firm's wider strategy | • managing partner may not be skilled in this activity<br>• may be defensive and not want to hear bad news<br>• client may object to this activity being used as an overt sales opportunity<br>• client may hold back with any one from the firm<br>• opportunity cost of fee earning vs. relationship management | Relationship management – opportunity to broaden and deepen the relationship if those opportunities are not being exploited effectively |

| | | | |
|---|---|---|---|
| Third party consultant | • shows investment from the firm<br>• interviews conducted by a skilled professional<br>• consistent approach<br>• rigorous analysis and reporting<br>• clients more forthcoming<br>• clients can interview a broad range of the firm's clients, spot trends and share market intelligence<br>• clients more willing to open up | • cost (although often outweighed by partners' time)<br>• learning curve – it is essential that consultants are well briefed | In-depth qualitative interviews regarding service delivery and future opportunities. Transaction reviews. Client audits. Can be specifically used for "problem children", "breadcrumb" clients and "silo" clients. Measure clients' perceptions and support branding projects. |

### Client listening framework

Whether you choose to conduct interviews over the phone, face-to-face or a combination of both, it's essential that you use your client's time well – so that they feel there is value for them in taking part. You need a framework for your client listening that provides the conversation with a structure and enables you to stay focused on the information you need from your client, even if the conversation moves off into other areas at various times. Your client listening framework should follow the following 6-point structure:

| | |
|---|---|
| **Managing service delivery** | • strengths<br>• weaknesses<br>• what needs to change |
| **Communications and relationships** | • responsiveness and proactivity<br>• consistency<br>• team<br>• changes |
| **Value** | • added value<br>• their strategic issues<br>• their challenges<br>• future changes in the business<br>• future requirements |
| **Brand perception** | • how do they perceive the brand?<br>• how does the brand value help/hinder?<br>• how is the brand valued against competitors? |
| **Competitors** | • strengths compared to other suppliers<br>• weaknesses compared to other suppliers |
| **Summary** | • summary of key outcomes<br>• actions required |

### Sample questioning framework

Set out below is a sample questioning framework which will enable you to explore the current situation and pinpoint areas for improvement, and also explore the future and identify potential opportunities.

## Client listening questions

### Introduction

- How long have you worked with people from [the firm]?
- How many people have you regularly worked for in that time?
- At what level are the people you work with?
- What projects have [the firm] worked with you on?

### Section 1 – Managing service delivery

- What are the firm's strengths?
- What do you really like about them?
    - Seek examples
- Are these your views or are they shared by colleagues?
- Is there anything you dislike about the firm?
- Does anything irritate you?
    - Seek examples
- Are these your views or are they shared by colleagues?
- Have colleagues shared any other views with you?
- Are there any examples of where the firm has failed to meet your expectations?
- Did you tell anyone and what did they do?
- Are there examples of where the firm has exceeded expectations?
- How do they compare with other firms you have used/use?
    - Seek examples of where good service delivery sets them apart or where competitors perform better.

### Section 2 – Communication and relationships

- In addition to this exercise how does the firm seek feedback from you?
- What changes have they made as a result of feedback?
    - Seek examples
- Are members of the team proactive?
    - Seek examples of where a member of the team has been proactive and the value for the client
- Is the firm responsive?
- Do you feel they are agile in responding to your needs?
- How could this be improved?
- Are you happy with the team doing your work?
- What changes, if any would you like to see?
- Are you happy with how the firm communicates in relation to progress on projects and costs?
- Does the team have a good understanding of your business and your market?
- How do they demonstrate this and use it for your benefit?
- Are there other stakeholders we should know?

**Section 3 – Brand**

- What is your perception of the [the firm] Brand?
- Do you see [the firm] as a company focused on the UK or a global brand which happens to operate in the UK market?
- What values would you attribute to the brand?
- What are their particular strengths/weaknesses?

**Section 4 – Value**

- What additional value do you get from the firm?
- Is there any additional value they could add to your business?
- What are the strategic issues on your agenda that are facing your business?
- Which are your priorities as a business?
- Do you feel the team is aware of your priorities?
- Have they discussed them with you?
- What business challenges do you face personally?
- Is there anything you would like to do for your customers and stakeholders that you are currently not doing?
- How effective is the firm in its use of innovation and thought leadership?
- How has this innovation and thought leadership helped to shape your requirements or change how you do things?
- What changes – if any – are you anticipating in your business in the next 12–24 months?
- Will any of these changes have an impact on your requirements from [the firm] in the future?
- What changes – if any – do you anticipate in your market/industry sector in the next 12 to 24 months?
- Do you feel the team is aware of these changes and their potential impact?
- Have they discussed them with you?

**Section 5 – Competitors**

- What are our strengths compared to other suppliers?
- What are our weaknesses compared to other suppliers?

**Section 5 - Summary**

- What are the firm's strengths/weaknesses compared to other company's you use for the same work?

**Section 6 – KPIs**

- **On a scale of 1 -10, how likely are you to recommend [the firm] to others?** (only 9s and 10s count. Scores of 1 – 6 are detractors. Scores of 7 and 8 are neutral in that they will say neither positive or negative things)
- **On a scale of 1 – 10, how well placed is [the firm] to support you to respond to future changes?**

**Getting started!**

Once you have agreed objectives for your client listening programme and agreed the most appropriate approach, it's time to get started. There are four essential parts to a client review process – **Preparation, Review, Feedback** and **Follow up.**

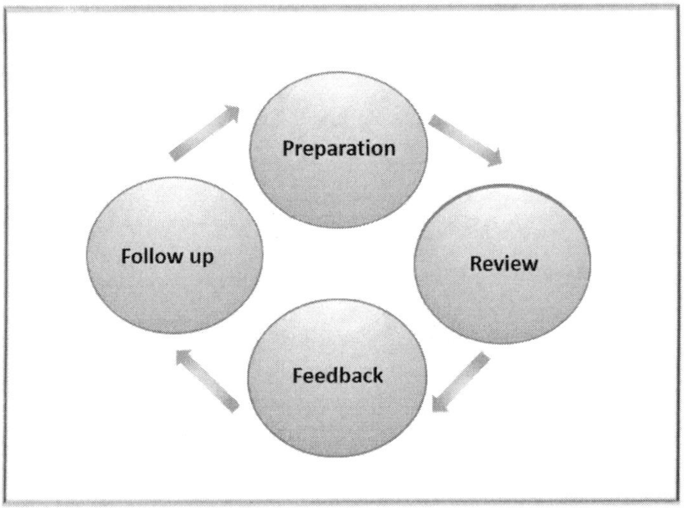


fig 23. Client listening framework

**Identify your target clients**

If you have not previously run a client listening programme or you feel you could build on what you currently do, the first job is to select the clients that you want to invite to take part. My suggestion is that you start small. This first group can effectively be your "proof of concept" from which you can make any tweaks before you roll it out to more clients. So, choose about –15 clients to start with. These may be your "top 10" clients, any "at risk", that you think may be in the zone of defection or "breadcrumb clients" that may be new or where you think there is good development opportunity. You may also want to include some referrers, as they are often a source of very useful insight on the views of clients.

**Preparation**

Once you have identified the clients you want to speak to, meet with the client team, or at least those individuals who have worked with them. Find out about the work that has been done in the past and any current work. Ask the client team about any major successes and any potential problem areas that the client may raise. Find out who the key stakeholders are that you should meet or speak to.

Remember in order to get an accurate picture of what is going on with the client, you may need to use a "multi-respondent" approach i.e. speak to or meet with a number of stakeholders in the client organisation. Finally, agree with the client team the areas you want to explore with the client and prepare a set of questions ahead of the meeting.

**Set up the meetings**

The next step is to get the meetings and/or calls booked in with clients. You need to send invites to clients, which sets out the purpose of your client listening exercise, asks for their contribution and explains that the person carrying out the review meeting will be in contact to arrange dates and times. Some client partners may prefer to speak to their client and invite them to take part, but in my view, this is risky for the person carrying out the review, as they won't know what has been said and will potentially go into the review unaware of the client's expectations.

**Review meeting**

Ensure you know your questions inside out, so that while the conversation has structure it still feels natural and not like an inquisition or a simple tick the box exercise. It's important to listen carefully to your client and if they express any dissatisfaction or concern, don't be tempted to justify or explain – the meeting may lose its legitimacy in the client's eyes and you may lose valuable insight. This is why it is better to use someone who is independent – whether it's someone from within the firm or an external consultant – to undertake the client listening, as they will remain objective throughout and allow the client to remain at the centre. Furthermore, an independent reviewer will be happy to ask the "difficult" questions.

Finally, if the client offers to take you round then take them up on it – it's fascinating and you'll learn loads more about the business.

**Debrief**

There is only one thing worse than not doing client listening and that is doing client listening and not acting upon the findings. Using an independent reviewer means they are less likely to "edit" the client's responses – either consciously or sub-consciously – and they will expect to report back promptly. The debrief, which should consist of a report and presentation, should take place within 1 week of the client meeting or call and should include everyone who works for the client. It is a good idea to get everyone from the client team together so that the feedback can be discussed and "next steps" agreed. There may be practical difficulties, especially if it is a large multi-site or multi-jurisdictional client team, in which case the next best thing is a conference call or video conference. When you have reviewed a large and complex client, the temptation is to simply send round the report for members of the client team to read and comment on. However, while this may overcome the practical difficulties of getting everyone together, it is not an effective way to debrief a client review meeting. There needs to be a common understanding of the client's feedback and agreement of the actions going forward. The risk in this situation is that nothing will happen.

Feedback from clients may well be both operational and strategic. In addition to debriefing the client team you may well need to have a debrief with the firm's leadership team on the strengths and weaknesses of the firm together with the opportunities and threats they may be exposed to. Firms that succeed in harnessing information at both the operational and strategic level to drive their client development strategies, will succeed in maximising the value from their client relationships.

**Getting the buy-in and overcoming resistance**

You may well experience some resistance to client listening and the principle reason for this is often fear – fear of what a client may say. I remember on one occasion suggesting to the managing partner of the firm I worked for that we should introduce client listening. *"Why do we want to do that?"* I was asked *"it'll just open a can of worms"*. Fear is also expressed as *"my clients will tell me if there is anything wrong" "my clients are very busy, they won't have time to do this"*. So, I suggest a simple change management approach.

1. Identify a senior and/or influential sponsor.
2. Don't boil the ocean – start small. Identify a group of "change agents" who you can work with on an initial client listening project – hopefully they will be working with clients that you want to target.
3. Prepare an internal comms programme to promote the client listening programme – including input from the senior sponsor.
4. Broadcast success.
5. Rollout the programme.

**Other client listening opportunities**

Throughout this chapter I have concentrated on how to run a formal client listening programme but we must not forget that some of the best client feedback may come over lunch or a glass of wine and it's important that we take up these opportunities to get feedback. Simple questions such as *"How did that last project go?", "Are you happy with how things are going?", "Is there anything we need to improve?",* can be very revealing. However, it is important this isn't just a "winking in the dark exercise" i.e. you do it, it makes you feel good but you then don't do anything. You need to make sure that any insights from clients is fed back into the overall client management strategy, to ensure you respond appropriately to what the client tells you.

# Chapter 14

## Maximising retention and revenue from existing clients

Exploiting the new business opportunities within existing clients is the most valuable and profitable source of new fees for any firm. Significant resources and effort often go into pursuing and winning new clients, while fees are effectively being left on the table with existing clients. According to Harvard Business Review, growing business and increasing revenue from existing clients, is five times cheaper than winning new clients, and other sources suggest it is even higher. Your major clients are often responsible for significant levels of fee income and profitability, and therefore it goes without saying that losing one of these clients could have a serious impact on your firm. In this chapter I will provide a practical guide to help you plan and implement your client development strategy, to profitably grow your fee income from existing clients.

Let's start by looking at the business imperative for developing your existing clients.

***Developing relationships with existing clients boosts client loyalty***

There are a number of very compelling reasons why prioritising your effort on developing existing clients will be a worthwhile and profitable strategy. Firstly, there is a direct relationship between client retention and profitability. Research by Bain & Co suggests that if you retain 5% of your clients, profitability will be boosted by anything from 25% to 90%.

***Pursuing business from existing clients has higher conversion rates***

The likelihood of converting business from existing clients is 60–70% but from new prospects it is 5–20% (Redwood analytics).

***Winning business from existing clients results in a greater share of their expenditure and reduces the risk of attrition.***

Increased levels of business – research shows that typically a firm can expect 23% of the business available but this can rise to 75% where there is a well-managed campaign to win business from other areas.

***Reduced attrition***

The less business you do with a client, the higher the rates of attrition (BTI Research). Typically, we see the following levels of attrition:

- 1 practice = 35% clients left the firm within 3 years
- 4 or more practices < 15% left the firm within 3 years
- 5 or more practices <10% practices left the firm within 3 years

If the client's main contact within a firm leaves then you may see attrition rates as follows:

- Single partner relationship – 72% clients would look for another firm
- Multi-partner relationship – 10% clients would look for another firm

None of this information will come as a surprise to anyone reading this. Yet despite these compelling reasons many professional firms could do a lot more to develop and grow their business from existing clients.

### Which clients?

Not all your clients will merit your investment, so the starting place is to identify those clients where there are opportunities to tap in to. Which clients will deliver a good return on your investment if you spend time developing them? Developing and implementing an effective client development strategy requires ongoing commitment and effort so you need to know you will see the rewards.

In chapter 2, I introduced **Accessibility and Attractiveness** as a model for helping you to target new clients. It is equally important that you apply the same rigour to identify which of your existing clients you want to develop.

### Selling beyond service

The first thing you need to do, if you want to grow the business you do with clients and increase revenues and profitability, is to change your mindset. You need to move beyond just thinking about "what additional services can I sell them?" to asking yourself "what's going on in this clients' business that I can help with?"

Many of the relationships that professional advisers have with their clients are "transactional" and "reactive" i.e. clients approach their adviser when they need something, and the professional adviser responds with whatever products or services are required. In between times there are varying degrees of social contact to nurture and embed the relationship and there may also be the delivery of a variety of added value services such as training or the provision of information. Selling at this transactional level focuses on delivering products and services as cheaply and efficiently as possible. If you want to maximise the revenue you get from a client you need to move beyond simply focusing on service delivery – you need to be looking at how you can help your client use your services better or how you can help them improve the efficiency of their processes and then look at the business as a whole to see how you can help them achieve their strategic objectives.

The example below shows how one firm grew their business, not by focusing on selling more services but on the strategic goals of the client and helping them to achieve that.

**A case in point...**

Redstone property LLP were the property managers for a landlord with a large and diverse property portfolio, consisting of retail, industrial and residential properties. They were responsible for property management across the entire portfolio. There KPIs were related to suppliers' costs for repairs and maintenance, minimising vacant periods, quality of tenants among other things. The business grew steadily as the portfolio grew.

However, the client did not instruct Redstone on anything other than property management, despite numerous attempts and introductions of other partners in the firm.

The client partner was keen to get the firm involved in other parts of the business, including the asset management side. He undertook a detailed review and valuation of the portfolio with one of his colleagues and identified that the capital value and yields were beginning to decline and forthcoming changes in legislation in the next 12 months could have an even greater impact on the overall value of the portfolio. They also felt that attracting the type of tenant the landlord wanted would become more difficult.

The client partner set up a meeting with the landlord and took him through the work they had done and made some suggestions about the longer-term management of his assets which would improve both the capital value and the yields. As a result, the landlord instructed the investment team at Redstone property LLP

**Make a plan**

If you want to leverage the full value from your clients in terms of growth and future revenues, you need to make a plan. Don't leave it to chance, because if you do, you're unlikely to get the work you want, and there's a risk your competitors may take your work.

*"Plan the work and work the plan"* – Margaret Thatcher

You don't need to overthink your plan or make it too complicated. It's easy to get bogged down in the process which will not serve you or your client well. The simpler your client development plan, the less likely it is to sit on your desk gathering dust and the more likely it will be to help you to meet your objectives.

Don't do your planning alone. Get together with your colleagues and other people you know who work with the client and who can make a valuable contribution. Whether or not there is a formally recognised client service team, there will be other people who may work with the client and can make a useful contribution to your plan.

## Diagnostic and planning tools

There are a number of very useful diagnostic and planning tools, described below, which will help you to be rigorous and thorough in planning your client development strategy.

### 1. Client overview

Begin your planning exercise with a detailed overview of your current relationship and what business you currently do with the client. If you have worked with the client for a number of years, then take an historical overview for the last 3 years to establish an accurate picture.

| **Product/Service** | **Revenue** | | |
|---|---|---|---|
| | **Year to date** | **2018/19** | **2017/18** |
| Support for lending – loan agreements etc. | **£ 400K** | **£ 100K** | **£ 50K** |
| Commercial contracts including supply agreements | **£ 100K** | **£ 0** | **£ 0** |
| Dispute management but not litigation | **£ 0** | **£ 0** | **£ 150K** |

### 2. SWOT analysis

SWOT analysis is a well-recognised tool used in any type of strategic planning exercise and you are probably familiar with it already. It is an extremely useful tool for answering the question "where are we now?" which is the starting place for developing your client development plan. In broad terms you need to ask the following questions:

1. What are the strengths of our relationship with this client? Where do we have competitive advantage we could build on?
2. What weaknesses are we aware of that we need to guard against in the future?
3. What opportunities exist for us to grow and expand our relationship with this client?
4. What threats exist that could damage or disrupt our relationship with this client?

You generally have more control over, and opportunity to act on internal factors such as strengths and weaknesses.

Opportunities and threats are external – these include market conditions, competitor activity, or something from within your client's organisation – and over which you have less control.

Remember that diagnostic exercises of this nature often raise more questions than answers but as I always say they are the right questions that will give you the information you need.

Here's an example of a typical SWOT analysis

| **Strengths – what you are good at** | **Weaknesses – what you are not good at** |
|---|---|
| We have a strong network of relationships with key stakeholders<br>We advise the CEO personally on tax matters<br>We manage their contracts database<br>They outsource a lot of their business services | Our last client listening highlighted a number of problems.<br>We only do one area of work and we are potentially pigeon-holed for that type of work<br>We only work for one division of the business<br>The client wants the work to be partner led but is reluctant to pay partner rates |
| **Opportunities – what you can take advantage of** | **Threats – what could be dangerous for you** |
| The client is very acquisitive<br>They operate in a growth market<br>They are reorganising their panel and procurement arrangements<br>A contact of ours from another client has recently joined the board | The work we do could easily be done in-house<br>They work with a number of our competitors<br>They are an attractive target for competitors<br>Our competitors work for other parts of the business<br>The head of department and our main contact day-to-day is leaving<br>They have a new head of procurement starting |

Having completed your SWOT analysis you need to decide what to do with the information you have gathered and in broad terms this is:

1. BUILD on your strengths
2. ADDRESS your weaknesses
3. PRIORITISE your opportunities
4. GUARD against your threats

### 3. Supply chain overview

A critical success factor in growing your clients and maximising revenues, is having a good understanding of their business, I think that a good place to start is to ensure you have a good understanding of your client's supply chain. The more you know about your client's supply chain, the more successful you will be at growing your business with that client. So, what is the supply chain and why is it important that we understand our client's supply chain?

The 'supply chain' is the network of people, organisations and systems that are involved in the transformation of raw materials into goods or services that are supplied to the end consumer. It includes parties inside and outside the organisation – suppliers, partner organisations, production and manufacturing, internal services units, distributors, retailers, transporters, and storage facilities that participate in the production, delivery and sale of a particular product or service.

The more you know about your client's supply chain, the greater will be your opportunity to create and deliver value to your client, which will lead to more business and a longer lasting relationship.

Whatever the nature of your client's business there are essentially 3 parts in their supply chain where there may be opportunities for you to help and support them:

- Purchasing
- Operations
- Distribution

This applies whether your client is a manufacturer, a service company or a public sector organisation.

A good place to start is to map out your client's supply chain – and you may need to do this in collaboration with your client. This will allow you to gain a detailed picture of how your client does business.

Invariably this exercise leads into a conversation around what challenges they are having with their supply chain or where problems in the supply chain may arise down the line.

Here are some questions you might ask to understand how your client's supply chain works and how you might be able to add some value.

## Purchasing

- Who are their suppliers?
- What goods and services do they buy-in?
- How do they source and select goods and services?
- How are these goods and services supplied?
- What are the KPIs

## Operations

- How do they transform the goods and services they buy-in to the goods and services they deliver to their customers?
- What resources do they need?
- Are these resources provided internally or externally?
- How are these goods and services stored?

## Distribution

- What does your client sell/deliver to their customers?
- How do they go to market?
- What resources do they use to sell/deliver to their customers?
- How do they manage those resources?
- What do their customers do with their goods and services?

Your services can be used at any part in this supply chain. How your client sees you is, to a large extent, dependant on your importance in their supply chain and the value you add as an individual or organisation. The harder you are to replace, the more important you will be to the client.

### 4. PEST analysis

PEST is a well-recognised and well-used strategic planning tool. It is also a very useful tool to help you plan your client development strategy, to help you analyse and understand the client's external environment. As with the supply chain overview, it will help you to pinpoint areas where you can add value to the client's business. The four **PEST** factors are:

- Political factors
- Economic factors
- Socio-cultural factors
- Technological factors

Here's an example of how you could use a PEST analysis to help you plan your client development strategy.

**Political – political factors which could impact your client's business**

Examples include – government policy, political stability, regulation, legislation, access to funds and grants, tax policy, immigration etc.

**Questions to ask**:

What changes in legislation or regulation may have an impact?

Is the political environment stable or likely to change and if so how?

Are there any factors that may provide opportunity for your client?

**Economic – economic forces which could impact your client's business**

Examples include – economic trends, industry trends, currency exchange rates, international trade arrangements, labour costs, consumer spending power, employment rates, inflation, interest rates, availability of credit, inflation etc.

**Questions to ask**:

What are the economic factors that may have an impact?

How does the performance of the economy affect the client at the moment?

What factors could provide your client with an opportunity?

**Social – social attitudes, behaviours and trends which could impact your client's business**

Examples include diversity, lifestyle trends, cultural and religious norms, changing values in the workforce e.g. attitudes of millennials, demographics

**Questions to ask**:

Are there any social or cultural trends which may have an impact on your client's business?

What opportunities are there for your client?

**Technological – technology which could affect how your clients makes, distributes and takes their products and services to market**

Examples include – emerging technology, automation, research and innovation, intellectual property regulations, technology and communications infrastructure

**Questions to ask**:

Are there any technological advances and innovations on the horizon which may impact our client?

How will this impact your client's business operations?

Are there any technology advances which will provide future opportunities?

The four quadrants in PEST vary in significance depending on your client's business.

**Go:Get analysis**

Within any client that you are actively developing, there may be several opportunities you want to pursue. Go:Get Analysis allows you to plot these opportunities and compare how likely you are to get each piece of business and its strategic value so that you can assess where you should focus your effort.

Go:Get analysis provides you with a visual map of your sales pipeline and helps you to monitor and manage the progress of opportunities through the sales pipeline.

There are two sets of criteria to help you analyse opportunities in the pipeline:

- How close is the client to a GO decision in relation to this particular opportunity? The measures for Go are the stages of the client's decision-making continuum (you will have read about the client's decision-making process in chapter 4)
- How likely are you to win this piece of business?

Here are the stages of GO:GET to help you analyse your opportunities:

| GO | GET |
|---|---|
| Living with changes (happy with the status quo) | Don't know the key decision-makers but competitors do |
| Awareness of problems | Our relationships are not with key decision -makers |
| Recognition of needs | We have good relationships with some key decision-makers but there are others involved that we don't know |
| Exploring options | Have a good relationship with key decision-makers but we know they are talking to competitors |
| Managing risk | Have a good relationship with key decision-makers and have helped to define needs |
| Decision is imminent | We have been told by key decision-makers that we are the preferred supplier |

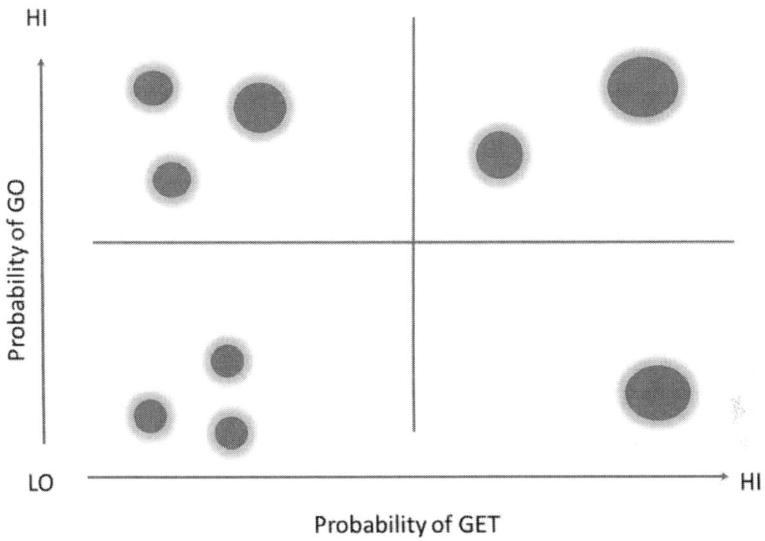


fig 24 Go.Get analysis

**Interpreting the matrix**

Ideally you will have a strong stream of bubbles moving from bottom left to top right. The things to look out for are:

- **Opportunities in the top left quadrant.**

A decision on these opportunities is likely (GO) but the chance of you winning the work is low (GET). In this case you need to think about how you can influence people to improve your chances of getting business.

Do you know enough people – if not can you contact other stakeholders?

Do you know people who can influence others on your behalf?

Are your competitors speaking to other stakeholders? Could this give them a competitive advantage?

- **Opportunities in the bottom right quadrant.**

The likelihood of the client making a decision is low (GO) but if they were to make a decision there is a high probability of you being instructed (GET). In this case you need to think about how you can influence more people to want what you are offering.

- Who else might be affected by the problems your solution will provide?
- Can you make the problems or opportunities you are dealing with bigger and more important for stakeholders?
- Are you working with other clients who have experienced the same difficulty and that you have helped?
- What outcomes have they seen?

- **Opportunities in the top right quadrant**

Don't take your eye off the ball. A high GO:GET score does not guarantee the business – keep an eye out for last minute problems that might mean you don't win the work.

- Are there stakeholders you don't know that are speaking to your competitors which could lead to a last-minute discussion to instruct them?
- Is there consensus among all the stakeholders?
- If not, could the decision be "put on hold"?

- **Opportunities in the bottom left quadrant.**

This part of the matrix should be full of opportunities. Any change inside or outside the business are triggers for change and are potential future opportunities. They should feature in the Go:Get matrix. For example, future legislative or regulatory changes may lead to opportunities or changes in personnel or corporate structures.

- What changes are there on the horizon that may give rise to future opportunities?
- What changes are we expecting/do we know about that might lead to new opportunities?
- What challenges are we seeing others in the sector focused on?
- Is there information we could get from their other advisers which might highlight opportunities?

### 5. Key Player map

In chapter 9, We explored the importance of understanding the various stakeholders who could make, influence and scrutinise decisions and to develop an effective stakeholder navigation strategy. A key part of your account development strategy is to prepare an accurate stakeholder or key player map and to plan your strategy to enhance your visibility and influence within the client organisation. You may want to refer back to the Power and Alignment model in chapter 9 and the indicators of power and alignment, to help you to do this.

When you are planning your stakeholder navigation strategy, there are two things you need to concentrate on:

- Getting to know the stakeholders/key players who make, influence and scrutinise decisions
- Establishing your competitive advantage with stakeholders/key players who can make, influence and scrutinise decisions

This is what will determine your stakeholder navigation strategy. Remember you need to establish an accurate picture of what is happening with various stakeholders. So, you may need to use other people you know inside and outside the client organisation to provide you with information.

The following table is a simple key player map I prepared for one of my consultancy clients. You will notice that there are some gaps in the information at this stage. As I have said previously these diagnostic activities often raise more questions than answers – but they are the right questions!

| Key player | Position | power/influence | alignment/support | stakeholder navigation strategy |
|---|---|---|---|---|
| Charlie Bird | HR Director | C-suite and actively involved. Likes to be seen as an innovator and driver of change and others listen to him. | Not known to us but may be known better by competitors, although there doesn't appear to be any one "favoured" supplier. | Invite to a forthcoming thought leadership seminar and introduce him to Tony (our CEO). |
| Helen Hope | Head of L&D | HH has been with the firm a long time. Regarded as a safe pair of hands. Goes with the flow a bit. Unlikely to "stick her neck out" – more inclined to stick with the status quo as long as it's working. HH has budgetary responsibility but devolves day-to-day responsibility to her team. | We've known HH a long time and she has always been very supportive of us. Not sure we have any particularly favoured position over other suppliers. I feel we are one of a number of suppliers they are happy to use. | HH has always been a strong advocate and happy to support us internally with other stakeholders. We know there are a number of people in the business interested in improving sales and negotiating capability so we need to use HH to support us. She has never seemed particularly sensitive or nervous about us having direct relationships with other stakeholders around the business. |
| Mary Smith | L&D manager | MS is quite new. We've met her and she has appointed us for a couple of small projects. At a project level she can decide who to use. Not sure if she can decide to bring in new suppliers. | I feel she is a bit of a "blocker". She has an internal training team which I think she would prefer to use. I think there are other suppliers she is closer to. She is not very accessible despite us being a long-standing supplier. | We need to stay in touch with MS to ensure we keep what we currently have. The likelihood of getting new projects from her is slim. New projects will come from other stakeholders. |

| Key player | Position | power/influence | alignment/support | stakeholder navigation strategy |
|---|---|---|---|---|
| Ellie Harry | Head of BD | EH is responsible for the key client programme. She has a dedicated team and budget responsibility. The key client programme is a board priority and they are making significant investment. We believe she has influence with the board. | We don't know EH. One of our team has worked on a project with one of her team in the past. We don't know which of our competitors she is close to, if at all? | We need to ask HH to make an introduction. Kelly in our team needs to re-engage with the person in EH's team that she has worked with in the past.<br>Invite EH to join the KAM breakfast club where we explore the latest research findings and insights on key client management.<br>Find out which of our competitors she is speaking to. |
| Ben Barker | COO | We have met a few times. He is seen as a driver of change and business improvement. He is leading on "project flight" to improve operating efficiency and profitability. He has budgetary responsibility. | BB knows our CEO from a previous role, and they have worked together on various projects in the past. He is interested in how we can help. | We need to involve our CEO in how we help BB on "project flight" and get HH to be our internal sponsor. HH made the original introduction so she will be happy to sponsor our involvement in "project flight" |

### 6. Competitor analysis

Earlier in the book, I introduced Decision Criteria, which is how clients and prospects compare and evaluate suppliers. Clients' Decision Criteria are the basis of your competitive advantage, so an important part of your client development strategy is to understand your clients' decision criteria

*"Poor firms ignore their competitors; average firms copy their competitors; winning firms lead their competitors." ~ Philip Kotler*

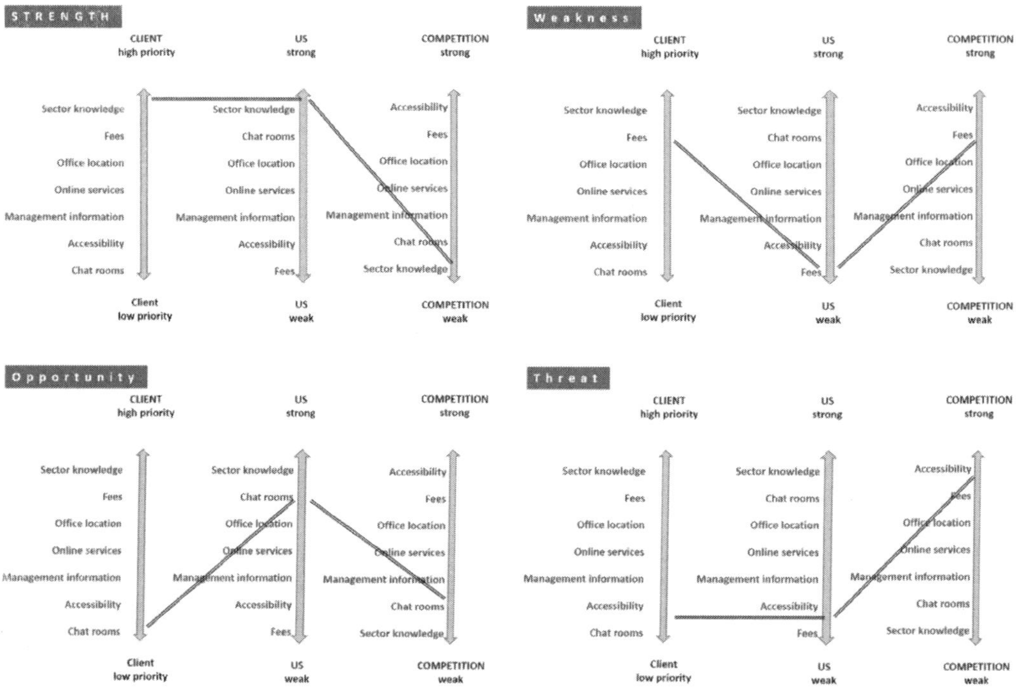


fig 25 - competitor analysis

Furthermore, there are various competitive selling strategies you can use to strengthen your competitive advantage:

***Strength***

In relation to crucial Decision Criteria (DC), the client sees you as stronger than competitors. The strategy here is to seek to reinforce your strengths to build competitive advantage.

*"As you quite rightly observe project management is very important to ensure you run transactions efficiently and don't run up unnecessary costs or miss deadlines. A number of clients have told us how user friendly and helpful our PM system is".*

***Weakness***

The client sees you as weaker than competitors in relation to crucial DCs. The strategy here is to redefine the DC so that you can meet the client's underlying need or to build up the importance of other DCs in the client's DCs.

*"I understand that the reason you want access to online information is because you have a young and relatively in experienced in-house team. We have run something called the Client Academy, which provides training, seminars etc – it is part of our education and support programme for clients".*

***Opportunity***

The client sees you as strong in relation to DCs which are not important to them. The strategy here is to build up the importance of the DC where you are seen as strong in order to gain competitive advantage.

*"We are finding that when clients adopt our transaction management programme, they are reducing costs by up to 20% and completing up to 90% of transactions on time".*

***Threat***

The client recognises competitors have strengths in relation to DCs that you don't – albeit in areas not important to them. Nevertheless, this is a potential risk and the strategy is to reinforce the areas where competitors are strong and are not important and build up the importance of other DCs where you are strong.

*"I must say that the clients we speak tell us that approach doesn't make a material impact on costs, however, transaction management can reduce costs by up to 20%".*

## Action plan

Having completed all your diagnostics using the tools I've described above, the final thing you need to do is to prepare an action plan. Here I want to highlight two things.

1. Don't "boil the ocean". Be realistic with what you can achieve. Too often I see individuals and client teams undertaking highly detailed and thorough planning exercises, the output of which is a very detailed action plan. Individuals then get involved in fee earning or other activities and action plans are then nothing more than a wish list. Once you have completed your planning exercise ask yourself "what can we realistically achieve in 100 days" and use that as the basis of your action plan – or at least your initial action plan.
2. Your plan needs to focus on outcomes not activities. I see many action plans which focus on activities e.g. attend client seminar, deliver training to client team, write article for client intranet, take client to the football. You will drive up revenues and grow the business you do with a client if you simply focus on activities but

fail to measure the outcomes you achieve. Your plan should include measures such as getting introductions to key stakeholders, meeting to discuss specific opportunities you have identified or challenges you know the client has, thought leadership events to meet key stakeholders, such as C-suite executives, meetings to introduce your colleagues to key stakeholders. We refer to these outcomes, where the client is willing to invest in the relationship as "lead indicators". There is a direct relationship between the number of lead indicators you get over a period of time and successful sales outcomes.

**Summary of what you have learnt in this chapter**

1. In this chapter, we explored the benefits to be gained by focusing on maximising revenues from existing clients.
    - **The cost of winning business** from existing clients is significantly cheaper than acquiring new clients.
    - **Rates of attrition materially reduce** when you broaden the range of services you provide because the relationship is more embedded and the value you provide is greater – in some cases business critical.
2. There are a number of diagnostic and planning tools that will help you develop your strategy for maximising revenue from existing clients.
    - **Client review** – to help you to build up a detailed picture of the business you currently do or have done in the past with a client.
    - **SWOT analysis** – a useful analytical tool in any planning exercise to help guide your strategy.
    - **PEST analysis** – a useful tool which helps you to analyse client's external environment and will help to pinpoint their challenges and priorities which will guide your client development strategy.
    - **Supply chain map** – a detailed understanding of the client's supply chain will help you to pinpoint where you can help. The more you can focus on helping clients achieve their strategic objectives and goals the more value you can deliver.
    - **Key player map** – to help you identify the key players/stakeholder who make, influence and scrutinise decisions and to plan your stakeholder navigation strategy, to enhance your influence within the client organisation.
    - **GO:Get analysis** – a tool that will enable you to identify, prioritise and manage a pipeline of opportunities within your client's business.
    - **Competitor analysis** – this tool will help identify the strengths and weaknesses of competitors, including internal teams, and help you plan your competitive selling strategy to gain competitive advantage. Finally, make sure your action plans are outcomes focused not activity focused.

## Terms and abbreviations used

| | |
|---|---|
| B2B | Business to Business |
| BD | Business Development |
| BLE | Board Level Executive |
| C-suite | A collective term for members of the board |
| CEB | Corporate Executive Board |
| DC | Decision Criteria |
| GCs | General counsel |
| L & D | Learning & Development |
| RFP | Request for Proposal |
| SLA | Service Level Agreement |
| VP | Value proposition |

## What next?

If you have read and enjoyed my book you may like to know how else I can help you.

I have a broad programme of training workshops, virtual classrooms and 1:1 sales mentoring designed to help individuals' and groups to develop their selling skills, to be even better at acquiring clients and winning business.

I also have a range of short podcasts and white papers covering various topics from my book.

I currently work with a number of professional service firms, including law firms, property companies, accountancy firms, advertising and marketing businesses and consultancy businesses, running a variety of face to face training programmes and virtual classrooms – particularly popular with international audiences!

Below is a list of my workshops – all of which can be tailored for the needs of individual clients.

- Networking skills
- Winning business through referrals
- Selling high value services
- Negotiating profitable fees
- Winning business in client meetings
- Dealing with procurement
- Finding and influencing decision makers (including getting access to the c-suite)
- Persuasive pitch presentations

However, if there is a particular topic you think I could help you with please contact me on my email. Information on all my training, virtual classrooms, podcasts and other resources to help you build your sales capability can be found on my website

katef@mobgroup.co.uk or visit our website www.mobgroup.co.uk